GET BY IN ENGLISH

4

Intermediate

コミュニケーションのための実践英語 4

［中級編］

Julyan Nutt
Michael Marshall
Yoko Kurahashi
Manabu Miyata

SANSHUSHA

音声ダウンロード＆ストリーミングサービス(無料)のご案内

http://www.sanshusha.co.jp/onsei/isbn/9784384335002/

本書の音声データは、上記アドレスよりダウンロードおよびストリーミング再生ができます。ぜひご利用ください。

Download

Streaming

Preface

Get By In English is a basic English conversation series aimed primarily at non-English majors. It has been produced largely with the needs of Japanese university students in mind, based on the writers' experience of what language is needed and what challenges Japanese university students face. The series is composed of four books: *Starter, Elementary, Pre-intermediate* and *Intermediate*.

Each textbook includes a variety of activities such as pair work, listening comprehension and grammar practice. Where necessary, time-saving explanations in Japanese have been given about the tasks they are required to do, and about some key language points to assist the students (and teachers). Another feature of the book is that students are encouraged, with the help of their teachers, to produce short speeches in English related to the topic of each particular unit.

Vocabulary has been chosen to reflect the needs of the students and comprehensive glossaries (English / Japanese and Japanese / English) are included in the text. In addition, there are optional interview test questions for teachers as a means of grading and monitoring students' progress. Over the 15-week course, students will build confidence in expressing themselves through conversations and speeches.

This book, *Intermediate*, is suitable for those students who are good at manipulating past continuous form, present perfect and other basic expressions, in addition to three simple tenses, present continuous form, or comparison. They are expected to learn such items as relatives, subjunctive mood, phrasal verbs and so on. As this is the fourth-level book, Japanese explanations are fewer than those given in the other three books. Also, students are required to write speeches with less help from their teachers.

本書の構成と特徴

本書は、Prefaceで述べましたように、『コミュニケーションのための実践英語』シリーズ4冊のうちの最後の4冊目にあたる中級編です。基本三時制や進行形・完了形あるいは比較構文などに習熟した学習者を想定しています。この中級編では、それらの用法や構文に加えて、関係詞や仮定法を用いた構文、句動詞の用法などを学ぶことになります。

本シリーズは、主として英語を専門としない学生を対象とした基礎的な英会話のテキストです。著者であるネイティブ・スピーカー2人が日本の大学生を教えてきた長

年の経験に基づき、大学生にとって必要とされるのはどのような英語か、また、どのような課題に直面しているかということを念頭において、編集されています。本書の構成を特徴とともに紹介すると、以下のようになります。

① 英語の授業を受ける際に必要となる最小限の表現と活動について学ぶためのWarm-up Unitから始めます。

② それに続く各ユニットを［Part A］と［Part B］に分け、［Part A］で基本となる語彙や表現を学び、［Part B］でそれを実際に用いる言語活動を行って、最後にスピーチで締めくくる、という構成になっています。

③ ［Part A］では、語彙の学習、発音とイントネーションの練習、モデルの対話文を用いた会話練習、文法問題、ペアで行う書き取り、と順に5つの段階を経て、必要な英語力を身につけます。

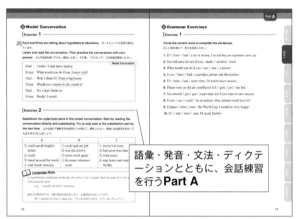

語彙・発音・文法・ディクテーションとともに、会話練習を行う**Part A**

④ ［Part B］では、リスニング問題に取り組みながら行う語彙の復習、ペアで行う会話練習、モデルとなるスピーチの学習、スピーチ原稿の作成、ペアの相手に行うスピーチ活動と、やはり順に5つの段階を経て、実践力を養います。

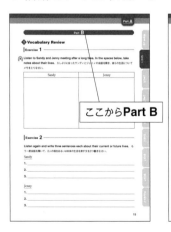
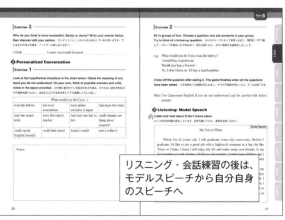

ここから**Part B**

リスニング・会話練習の後は、モデルスピーチから自分自身のスピーチへ

⑤３つのユニットを終えると、復習のためのReview Unitがあります。それまでの学習の成果を測るために、担当の先生が個人面接をする際にたずねる質問を想定した"Interview Test Questions"が最初に設けてありますので、先生の質問に答える準備をしてください。これに続く、適語選択問題、英文完成問題、並べ替え問題、質問文作成問題、読解問題は、クラスメートが面接を受けている間に各自で取り組むこととなります。

⑥最初のReview Unit 1が終わると、同じように３つのユニットとReview Unit 2で学習します。こうして、Warm-up Unitに授業１回分（＝90分）、各ユニットに授業２回分（計12回）、Review Unitに２回分という具合に、15回分の学習内容が１冊に収めてあります。

⑦本書では、与えられたタスクの内容や文法に関する重要なポイントについて、日本語による説明が加えてありますが、中級レベルの学習者を意識して、必要最小限に抑えてあります。

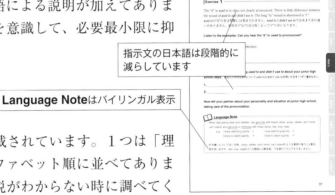

指示文の日本語は段階的に
減らしています

Language Noteはバイリンガル表示

⑧巻末に、２種類の索引が掲載されています。１つは「理解のための語彙」で、アルファベット順に並べてあります。各ユニットの英文や解説がわからない時に調べてください。もう１つは「発話のための語彙」で、ペア活動の際に役立つ語彙を、トピック別にアイウエオ順にまとめました。日本語に相当する英語がわからない時に活用してください。

　本書を用いた学習で、大学生として必要とされる英会話力がつくことを願っています。

　　　　　　　著者一同

英和形式
ABC順語彙集

和英形式
トピック別語彙集

Table of Contents

Welcome to English Class!

◆1 Classroom English

In English class, try to speak English as much as possible. Here are some useful questions or expressions. 授業中にはできる限り英語で話すようにしなさい。よく使う表現を覚えましょう。

| Exercise 1

Read the following dialogues. Choose the correct sentences from the box.
次の会話の空所になっている箇所に次ページの一覧表から適する表現を選んで入れなさい。

1. Teacher: Now, can you turn to page 105?

Student : _____

Teacher: Sorry, ... Turn to... page ... one hundred... and... five.

Student : _____

Teacher: Sure, ... Page... one hundred... and... five.

2. Student : _____

Teacher: That's adjective.

Student : _____

Teacher: A, D, J, E, C, T, I, V, E.

3. Student : _____

Teacher: SYL – la – ble.

Student : Thank you.

4. Student : _____

Teacher: It means an extra question.

Student : Oh, I see. Thanks.

5. Student: _____

Teacher: Sure, go ahead.

Student: When is the end of term test?

Teacher: In two weeks. On January 25th.

6. Student: _____

Teacher: Yes, but please put it in your bag when you have finished.

Student: Okay, I will.

7. Student: _____

Teacher: Yes. How can I help?

Student: _____

Teacher: Of course, I'll play it again.

01

May I ask a question?	Can we listen to that again?
May I use my *smartphone dictionary*?	Please say that again.
How do you pronounce this word?	Please speak more slowly.
How do you say 形容詞 in English?	Excuse me! (*To call the teacher, you can raise your hand and say, 'Excuse me!'*)
How do you spell *adjective* (*that*)?	
What does *follow-up question* (*this word*) mean?	

Exercise 2

Practice the conversations with your partner. One of you plays the role of teacher, the other the student. Now change roles. ペアの相手と教師役・学生役を交替しながら、**Exercise 1**で完成した会話を練習しなさい。

Language Note

In English, it is usually natural to use the teacher's name like "Mr. Smith" or "Ms. Hayashi," not say "Teacher." Use the name the teacher asks you to use.

英語で先生に話しかける時には、"Teacher"とは言いません。"Mr. Smith"とか"Ms. Hayashi"のように、先生の名前を言うのが普通です。先生が指示する言い方で呼びかけるようにしなさい。

❷ Practice patterns

1) **Read the practice explanations in both English and Japanese. Choose the practice pattern from the box and write it in the correct place.** 英語と日本語の練習の説明を読んで、選択肢から練習の型を選び、適した場所に記入しなさい。

Practice Patterns

The followings are typical Practice Patterns in this class.

Five-finger Challenge	Changing Partners
Read, Remember, Repeat	Key Point Shadowing

1. _____	2. _____
Students practice a dialog, but do not read the dialog directly. Each line they read to themselves, and remember it. Then repeat without looking. The aim is to learn (memorize) the dialog pattern. 会話文を読まないで、会話の練習をしなさい。まず、黙読して覚えなさい。つぎに、見ないで会話文を繰り返しなさい。この練習の目的は会話のパターンを学ぶことです。	Students have a conversation. Each time they speak, they count one finger. Once both students have counted five times, the challenge is complete. 英語で会話をします。会話をするたびに、指を使って数えなさい。2人が5回ずつ数えたら、練習は終了です。(5回の取り組み)
3. _____	4. _____
One student listens carefully to the other. They then try to repeat the key point that they hear. 相手の言うことをよく聞きます。つぎに聞こえたキーポイントを繰り返します。	After each exercise, half of the class should move seats and find a new partner. The next week, the other half of the class will move. 練習が終わるたびに、クラスの半数が席を移動して新しいペアの相手と組みます。翌週は他の半数が移動します。

❸ Nice to meet you!

Exercise 1

Complete the answers with information about yourself.

まず、次の質問に答えて"**Myself**"の欄に記入しなさい。

	Myself	My partner
Where are you from?	I'm from _____	_____
Where do you live?	I live in _____	_____
What do you do?	I'm a _____	_____
What's your major?	My major is _____	_____
What do you do in your free time?	I like to _____ in my free time.	_____
Do you have a part-time job?	Yes, _____ No, I don't.	_____
How many hours a week do you work?	I work _____ hours a week.	_____
When's your birthday?	My birthday is on _____	_____
How do you come to college?	I come to college by _____	_____
How long does it take you to come to college?	It takes about _____	_____

Exercise 2

Now ask your partner the questions.

つぎにペアの相手に質問し、その答えを"**My partner**"の欄に記入しなさい。

Exercise 3

Change partners and take turns asking your new partner the questions.

別のペアになり、新しいパートナーと質問し合いなさい。

Exercise 4

Tell your new partner about your previous partner.

新しいパートナーに前のパートナーから聞いたことを伝えなさい。

Unit 1
Unit 2
Unit 3
Review 1
Unit 4
Unit 5
Unit 6
Review 2

Language Note

When you are asked a "Do you.....?" question, it is grammatically correct to just answer "Yes" (Yes, I do) or "No" (No, I don't). However, in real conversations, it is more common (and polite!) to answer by giving a little more information.

> e.g.　A: "Do you have a part-time job?"
>
> 　　　B: "Yes. I work in a supermarket."

"Do you.....?"とたずねられた時、単に"Yes"（Yes, I do）とか"No"（No, I don't）とだけ答えても、間違いではありません。しかし、実際の会話では、上の例にあるように、もう少し情報を添えるのが普通で、丁寧な答え方になります。

"What do you do?" does not mean "What are you doing?" In English, asking *What do you do?* is more natural than asking *What is your job?*

"What do you do?"は「今、何をしていますか？」という意味ではありません。相手の職業を聞く場合、What do you do?はWhat is your job?よりも自然な表現なのです。

Note on speeches

From Unit 1 you will prepare and make short speeches in English. The textbook will give you advice and hints about what to write. Ask your teacher for help if you need it. （Don't be shy!） You will read your speech to your conversation partner. You will also listen to other students' speeches. Writing and reading speeches aloud will help you practice your English more. Good luck!

スピーチについて

次のユニットから、英語で短いスピーチをすることになります。スピーチについてのヒントや助言はテキストにありますが、必要に応じて先生にたずねてください。恥ずかしがらずに聞くことです。準備ができたら、パートナー相手にスピーチしたり、逆に相手のスピーチを聞いたりします。スピーチ原稿を書いたり、読んだりすることは、とても良い練習になります。成功を祈ります！

> Enjoy your class!
> 授業を楽しみましょう！

Do you have any dreams for the future?

Part **A**

1 Warm Up: Key Vocabulary

Exercise 1

Choose a verb from the box to complete the phrases. More than one answer is possible. 下の語句を完成するために表から適する動詞を選んで記入しなさい。答えが1つとは限りません。

be / become / get / have / live / make / own / start / study / travel

1. _____ a business
2. _____ married
3. _____ a family
4. _____ abroad
5. _____ a good job

6. _____ around the world
7. _____ a nice car
8. _____ successful
9. _____ a lot of money
10. _____ famous

Imagine you are thirty years old. What would your ideal life be?

Choose phrases from above or your original ideas to complete five sentences about yourself.

あなたが30歳になった時の理想的な人生がどのようなものかを想像して、5つの文を作りなさい。

Exercise 1の語句から選んでも、自分で考えた語句を使ってもかまいません。

e.g. I would live in a large house in the country.
      I would be married with two children.

      What would your ideal life be?

1. I would _____.

2. I would _____.

3. I would _____.

4. I would _____.

5. I would _____.

Now ask your partner.

では、パートナーに質問しなさい。

Exercise 3

Change partners and tell your new partner five things you found out about your previous partner. 別のペアになり、最初のパートナーについて5つのことを伝えましょう。

Language Note

When discussing hypothetical situations—those that are not real or are unlikely to happen—we use *would + verb*. When discussing situations that are likely to happen, we use *will + verb*.
現実的でない、あるいは起こりそうにもない仮定の状況を語る時、*would* + 動詞を使用します。起こりそうな状況を語る時には、*will* + 動詞を使用します。

❷ Pronunciation

| Exercise 1

Depending on where people are from, native speakers of English sometimes pronounce words differently.

The linked part of *would you, could you* or *should you* can either be pronounced *~dju* or *~dja*.

出身地により、英語のネイティブ・スピーカーの発音が異なることがあります。*would you*、*could you*、あるいは*should you*の連結した部分は~dju、あるいは~djaと発音されます。

Examples

1. Would you do me a favor? → Woul**dju** do me a favor?
2. Where would you live? → Where woul**dja** live?
3. Could you tell me your name? → Coul**dya** tell me your name?
4. Would you do that, if you were me? → Woul**dyu** do that, if you were me?

| Exercise 2

Rewrite the sentences from Warm-up Exercise 2 as Yes/No questions.

Warm-upの**Exercise 2**で作った5つの文をYes/Noで答える疑問文に書き換えなさい。

1. Would you _____ ?
2. _____ ?
3. _____ ?
4. _____ ?
5. _____ ?

| Exercise 3

Change partners and find out if your new partner's dream life would be similar to yours, taking care with the linked sounds.

別のペアになり、新しいパートナーの理想の人生があなたの理想の人生と似ているかどうかを確かめなさい。つなげて発音する部分に注意しなさい。

❸ Model Conversation

Exercise 1

05 **Paul and Erina are talking about hypothetical situations.** ポールとエリナは仮定の話をしています。

Listen and read the conversation. Then practice the conversation with your partner. 2人の会話を聞いてから、音読しなさい。その後、ペアになって、この会話を練習しなさい。

Model Conversation
Paul : I wish I ①had more money.
Erina: What would you do if you ②were rich?
Paul : Well, I think I'd ③buy a big house.
Erina: Would you ④move to the country?
Paul : No, I don't think so.
Erina: Really? I would.

Exercise 2

Substitute the underlined parts in the model conversation. Start by reading the conversation directly and substituting. Try to only look at the substitution part by the last time. 上の会話の下線部を次の語句に入れ替えて、練習しなさい。最後には会話文を見なくても言えるようにしましょう。

A	B	C
① could speak English better	① could quit my job	① weren't so busy
② could	② won the lottery	② had more free time
③ travel around the world	③ never work again	③ relax more
④ visit South America	④ do some volunteer work	④ stay home and watch Netflix

📖 **Language Note**

In hypothetical conditional sentences, the verb in the *if* clause takes the past form; the *be* verb becomes *were*.

　　　e.g.　I wouldn't do that if I were you.

仮定法の条件文では、*if*節の動詞は過去形となり、be動詞は*were*となります。

　　　例）I wouldn't do that if I were you. （もし私があなたなら、そうしないでしょう。）

④ Grammar Exercises

Exercise **1**

Circle the correct word to complete the sentences.
正しい語を選んで、英文を完成しなさい。

1. If I (have / had) a lot of money, I would buy an expensive new car.

2. You will pass the test if you (study / studied) hard.

3. What would you do if you (see / saw) a ghost?

4. If you (have / had) a question, please ask the teacher.

5. If I (have / had) more time, I'd watch more movies.

6. Please turn on the air conditioner if it (gets / got) too hot.

7. You should (get / got) a part-time job if you want to save money.

8. If you (can / could) be an animal, what animal would you be?

9. If Japan (wins / won) the World Cup, I would be very happy!

10. If I (was / were) you, I'd study harder.

Exercise 2

Complete the sentences *using your own ideas*. Be careful to use the correct form of the verbs.

あなたの考えで次の文を完成しなさい。動詞の形に注意しましょう。

1. I would be very surprised if _____ .

2. If it rains tomorrow, _____ .

3. If _____ , please call the police.

4. If I were very rich, _____ .

5. If I lived abroad, _____ .

6. If _____ , I would be very happy.

7. If you are sick, _____ .

8. If I lost my cellphone, _____ .

9. If I weren't a student, _____ .

10. Don't _____ if you have influenza!

⑤ Pair Dictation

Student A: Turn to page 93.

Aさん：93ページを見なさい。

Student B: Turn to page 103.

Bさん：103ページを見なさい。

1 Vocabulary Review

Exercise 1

Listen to Sandy and Jenny meeting after a long time. In the spaces below, take notes about their lives. 久しぶりに会ったサンディとジェニィの会話を聞き、彼らの生活についてメモをとりなさい。

Sandy	Jenny

Exercise 2

Listen again and write three sentences each about their current or future lives. もう一度会話を聞いて、2人の現在あるいは未来の生活を表す文を3つ書きなさい。

Sandy

1. _____
2. _____
3. _____

Jenny

1. _____
2. _____
3. _____

Exercise 3

Who do you think is more successful, Sandy or Jenny? Write your answer below, then discuss with your partner. サンディとジェニィのどちらが成功していると思いますか。下にあなたの考えを書き、パートナーと話し合いなさい。

I think _____ is more successful because _____

❷ Personalized Conversation

Exercise 1

Look at the hypothetical situations in the chart below. Check the meaning of any word you do not understand. On your own, think of possible answers and write notes in the space provided. 次の表に書かれている仮定の状況を読み、分からない語句があればその意味を調べなさい。自分ならどうするかを考えて下の空欄にメモしなさい。

What would you do if you...?			
won the lottery	lost your smartphone	were prime minister of Japan	had more free time
had one magic wish	were this class's teacher	had only one day to live	could change one thing about yourself
could speak English fluently	could time travel	found a wallet	saw a robbery

Notes:

Exercise **2**

Sit in groups of four. Choose a question and ask someone in your group.
Try to think of a follow-up question. 4人のグループになって着席しなさい。質問を1つずつ選んで、グループの誰かにたずねなさい。答えを聞いたら、それに関連する質問をしましょう。

e.g. What would you do if you won the lottery?
I would buy a sports car.
Would you buy a Ferrari?
No, I don't think so. I'd buy a Lamborghini.

Cross off the question after asking it. The game finishes when all the questions
have been asked. たずね終わった質問は消しなさい。すべての質問が終わったら、ゲームは終了です。

Hint: Use Classroom English if you do not understand and be careful with linked sounds.

❸ Listening: Model Speech

Listen and read about Eriko's future plans.
エリコが将来計画の話をしています。音声を聞いてから、原稿を音読しなさい。

Model Speech

My Future Plans

When I'm 22 years old, I will graduate from this university. Before I graduate, I'd like to get a good job with a high-tech company in a big city like Tokyo or Osaka. I hope I will enjoy city life and make many new friends. In my late twenties or early thirties, I'd like to get married. I might have children, but I haven't decided yet. Even if I have children, I don't want to quit my job. I will work hard and try to save a lot of money.

In my thirties, if I have enough money, I'd like to quit my job and start my own technology business. I'd like to make a lot of money, but I also want to enjoy my work. If I am successful, I will probably retire early, maybe around 60. I would like to build my own house and live in the countryside or by the sea. I might do some volunteer work sometimes. Also, when I am retired, I want to travel around the world and visit many countries. I will need to speak English, so I will not stop studying English after graduation!

④ Personalized Speech

Write a speech. Introduce yourself, then write about your future plans.

あなたの将来計画に関するスピーチ原稿を書きなさい。

⑤ Speech: Pair Discussion

Exercise 1

Now work in pairs. Read your speech to your conversation partner. Listen carefully to your partner's speech.

ペアになってスピーチ原稿を読み、相手に聞いてもらいなさい。交替して、相手のスピーチをしっかり聞いてあげましょう。

Exercise **2**

Ask your partner questions. First, write 3 follow-up questions.

例にならって、ペアの相手にたずねる質問を3つ書きなさい。すでにスピーチで聞いたことを質問しないように注意しましょう。

Examples of questions:

What (kind of) job do you want to get after graduation?

Do you want to get married in the future?

Do you think you will _____?

MY QUESTIONS

1. _____?

2. _____?

3. _____?

Exercise **3**

Now ask your questions.

Exercise **4**

Take two minutes to memorize your speech. Then, close the textbook and try to make the speech again. (It is not important to repeat your speech perfectly, just try to remember as much as you can!) 2分でスピーチを覚えなさい。覚えたら、テキストを閉じてもう一度スピーチをしなさい。(完璧なスピーチでなくてもかまいません。できる限り見ないで言えるようにしましょう。)

Are you feeling okay?

Part **A**

❶ Warm Up: Key Vocabulary

Exercise **1**

Match the health problems with phrases from the box.

絵に描かれた健康問題と下の語句とを結びつけなさい。

(　) an earache	(　) a fever	(　) break (an) arm	(　) depressed
(　) a headache	(　) a cough	(　) sprain (an) ankle	(　) insomnia
(　) a toothache	(　) a cold	(　) twist (a) finger	(　) overweight
(　) a stomachache	(　) the flu	(　) hurt (a) knee	(　) stressed

a.

b.

c.

d.

e.

f.

g.

h.

i.

j.

k.

l.

m.

n.

o.

p.

Exercise 2

Using phrases from the box, describe what you would do if you had some of the health problems above. あなたが**Exercise 1**にあるようなことになったらどうするかを、下の語句を用いて書きなさい。

Remember these are hypothetical situations, so use: *If + would.*

(09) e.g.　If I had a sprained ankle, I would go to the hospital.
　　　If I had a toothache, I would put up with it.
　　　If I were depressed, I would speak to a friend.

go to the hospital	put up with it
go to the dentist	put it in cold water
go to bed early	wrap a bandage around it
take some medicine	stay home and rest
speak to someone	go to the gym

1. If I _____, I would _____.

2. If _____.

3. _____

4. _____

5. _____

Exercise 3

When was the last time you were really ill? What happened and what did you do? Write three sentences explaining the situation. 最近、実際に具合が悪くなったのはいつですか。どうなって、何をしましたか。その状況を説明する文を3つ書きなさい。

_____

_____

_____

Exercise 4

Tell your partner about the situation in Exercise 3. Try not to read what you wrote. When your partner tells you their situation, can you think of follow-up questions and ask them?

❷ Pronunciation

Exercise 1

Often native speakers do not clearly pronounce the final *t* sound at the end of a word, especially in casual conversation.

ネイティブ・スピーカーは単語の最後にくる *t* の音をはっきりと発音しないことが、特に日常会話で多くなります。

 e.g.　What were you doing last night?　　Not much. I was at home.
　　　　Wha' were you doing las' nigh'?　　No' much. I was a' home.

Listen to the dropped 't' in the following sentences.

1. I got home at eight.　　　　→　I go' home a' eigh'.
2. I didn't do that.　　　　　　→　I didn" do tha'.
3. It starts just after nine.　　→　I' starts jus' after nine.
4. I can't get there before ten.　→　I can' ge' there before ten.
5. That's not right.　　　　　　→　Tha"s no' righ'

Exercise 2

Practice asking and answering the questions with your partner. Remember, people drop *t* because it is easier to say. It sounds strange if you pause in the sentence. Try "Read, Remember, Repeat."
Think about pronunciation, stress and intonation, then say.

❸ Model Conversation

Exercise 1

🎧 11 **Yumi is worried about Greg.**

Listen and read the conversation. Then practice the conversation with your partner.

> Model Conversation
>
> Yumi: Are you okay?
>
> Greg: Not really. ①I think I have a cold.
>
> Yumi: If I were you, I would ②go to the doctor.
>
>   You might ③have the flu.
>
> Greg: No, I don't want to do that.
>
> Yumi: Well, you'd better ④go home and rest then.
>
> Greg: Yeah, you're probably right.

Exercise 2

Substitute the underlined parts in the model conversation. Start by reading the conversation directly and substituting. Try to only look at the substitution part by the last time.

A	B	C
① my foot hurts	① I can't sleep recently	① my mouth hurts
② speak to the coach	② speak to the school	② go to the dentist
③ have sprained your counselor		③ have a toothache
ankle	③ be depressed	④ put up with it
④ wrap a bandage around	④ exercise outside more	
it		

4 Grammar Exercises

Exercise 1

Match the following sentences (1-10) with the advice below (a-j). Write the correct words in the space. (More than one answer may be possible.)

1. I feel tired. ( )

2. I'm hungry. Let's eat lunch somewhere. ( )

3. I have a toothache. ( )

4. I want to quit college! ( )

5. I need to save money for my summer vacation. ( )

6. What shall we do tomorrow? ( )

7. I can't wake up early, so I'm often late for class. ( )

8. When is a good time to visit Kyoto? ( )

9. Can we use our smartphones in class? ( )

10. I want to be a good English speaker. ( )

Hints : Don't ~	How about ~	If I were you ~
Why don't you ~	You should ~	You shouldn't ~

a) _____ going to that new Italian restaurant?

b) _____ get a part-time job.

c) Maybe autumn. _____, I wouldn't go in the summer. It's too hot.

d) _____ call or mail, but you can use the Internet to check something.

e) _____ take a rest?

f) _____, I'd go abroad and do a homestay.

g) _____ going to the art museum? It looks interesting.

h) _____ give up! Your parents would be very disappointed.

i) _____ go to the dentist as soon as possible.

j) _____ go to bed so late at night.

Exercise 2

Write the sentences or questions in the correct order. Then match them to the replies below (a-e).

1. were / you / would / I / English / if / dramas / more / watch / I

_____. (   )

2. Italy / year / to / how / next / going / about

_____? (   )

3. up / give / don't

_____! (   )

4. should / now / do / we / what

_____? (   )

5. much / weight / you / if / shouldn't / want / lose / so / to / eat / you

_____. (   )

a) I know, but it's difficult. I love Italian pasta so much!

b) I don't know. Maybe watch a movie?

c) OK. Thanks. I'll do my best.

d) Really? Is that a good way to improve my listening?

e) That's a good idea. I've never been there before.

5 Pair Dictation

Student A: Turn to page 94.   **Student B: Turn to page 104.**

① Vocabulary Review

| Exercise 1 ─────────────────────────

(12) **Lucy is visiting the school nurse to discuss some of the problems she is having. What health problems does Lucy have? Listen to the conversation.** ルーシーは、悩んでいる問題について相談しようと、大学の保健師さんのところに来ています。ルーシーはどんな問題を抱えていますか。

Health Problems	Advice
1. _____	1. _____
2. _____	2. _____
	3. _____
	4. _____
	5. _____
	6. _____

| Exercise 2 ─────────────────────────

Listen again. What advice does the school nurse give her?

| Exercise 3 ─────────────────────────

Do you agree with the school nurse? If you were the nurse, what advice would you give Lucy?

Remember to use *would* with hypothetical situations.

_____

_____

② Personalized Conversation

Exercise 1

Look at the health problems in the chart below. On your own, think of advice you could give for each health problem and write notes in the space provided.

e.g. *If I were you, I would* go to the hospital.
You should go to the hospital.
Why don't you go to the hospital?
How about going to the hospital?

Health Problems			
a headache	twisted finger	depressed	a cold
broken arm	a toothache	back hurts	an earache
the flu	a stomachache	sprained ankle	overweight
stressed	hurt knee	a cough	insomnia

Notes:

Language Note

The advice *How about~?* uses the gerund; *If I were you, you should~*, and *Why don't you~?* use the plain form of the verb.

How about~? と助言する場合、*How about* の後には動名詞を用います。*If I were you, you should ~* と *Why don't you ~?* では、動詞の原形を用います。

31

Sit in groups of four. Choose a health problem and ask all the other members of the group for different advice.

Decline the first two, then accept the final piece of advice.

e.g. A: I have a stomachache. What should I do?

        B: Why don't you speak to a doctor?

        A: No, I don't want to do that.

        C: How about taking some medicine?

        A: No, I don't want to do that, either.

        D: You should put up with it then.

        A: Yeah, you're probably right.

Cross off the health problem each time. The game finishes when all the problems have been discussed.

Hint: Use **Classroom English** if you do not understand and be careful with linked sounds.

3 Listening: Model Speech

🎧 13 **Listen and read about what Masaru would do if he won the lottery.**

Warm-up
Unit 1
Unit 2
Unit 3
Review 1
Unit 4
Unit 5
Unit 6
Review 2

> Model Speech
>
> If I Won the Lottery
>
> Recently I bought a lottery ticket at my local shopping mall. The top prize is ¥100,000,000! That is a lot of money! I have been thinking how I would use the money if I won the top prize.
>
> If I won the lottery, first I would have a big party to celebrate and would invite all my friends. Also, I would quit my part-time job because I wouldn't need the money and it's a little boring! However, I wouldn't quit university and I might even study harder than now because I would have more time.
>
> I would buy many things with the money. I'd like to buy a small apartment and a sports car. I'd also take a trip around the world. In addition, I would give some of the money to my parents who have worked very hard to help me. Of course, I wouldn't spend all the money. I would save a lot of money in the bank.
>
> Some people say that, if they won the lottery, they would never work again, but I think I would do something, maybe volunteer work or try to start some interesting business. I know this is probably just a dream. For now, I will continue my normal life, study and do my part-time job.

4 Personalized Speech

Imagine if you won the lottery and write a speech about what you would do with the money.

_____

_____

_____

_____

_____

_____

_____

_____

_____

_____

_____

⑤ Speech: Pair Discussion

Exercise 1

Now work in pairs. Read your speech to your conversation partner. Listen carefully to your partner's speech.

Exercise 2

Ask your partner questions. First, write 3 follow-up questions.

Examples of questions:

Would you still work if you won the lottery?

What is the first thing you would buy?

How much money would you save?

MY QUESTIONS

1. _____ ?

2. _____ ?

3. _____ ?

Exercise 3

Now ask your questions.

Exercise 4

Take two minutes to memorize your speech. Then, close the textbook and try to make the speech again. (It is not important to repeat your speech perfectly, just try to remember as much as you can!)

Unit 3

What were you like in junior high?

Part A

1 Warm Up: Key Vocabulary

Exercise 1

Match the personality type to the picture.

( ) shy	( ) smart	( ) kind
( ) hardworking	( ) outgoing	( ) lazy
( ) cute	( ) funny	( ) naughty
( ) athletic	( ) creative	( ) ambitious
( ) competitive	( ) musical	( ) talkative

a.  b.  c.

d.  e.  f.

g.  h.  i.

j.  k.  l.

35

m.    **n.**   **o.**

Exercise 2

When you were at junior high school, what were you like? Write a sentence using *used to*, and a follow-up sentence explaining in more detail. あなたがどんな中学生だったかについて、used toを用いて書きなさい。それに続いて詳しく説明する文を書きましょう。

e.g.   I used to be shy but hardworking.   I used to be quite athletic.
        I spent a lot of time studying in the   I was always outside playing
        library by myself.   sports.

Used to: _____

Explanation: _____

Language Note

The term *used to~* describes something that was true in the past but not in the present. Conversely, *didn't use to~* describes something that was not true in the past but is in the present.

*used to~*は過去にそうであったが、現在はそうでないことを述べるときに使用します。逆に、*didn't use to~*は過去にはそうでなかったが、現在ではそうであることを述べるときに使用します。

Exercise 3

Change partners and without saying anything, guess what they used to be like and write your reason. 別のペアになり、新しいパートナーがどんな中学生だったかを想像し、その理由とともに書きなさい。話してはいけません。

Used to: I think you used to be _____

Explanation: _____

When you have both finished, tell each other your guesses. Were you correct?

❷ Pronunciation

Exercise 1

The "d" in *used to* is often not clearly pronounced. There is little difference between the sound of *used to* and *didn't use to*. The long "to" sound is shortened to "t".

*used to*の"d"の音は明瞭には発音されません。*used to*と*didn't use to*ではあまり音の違いがありません。長母音の"to"の音は短くなって"t"の音になります。

Listen to the examples. Can you hear the "d" in *used to* pronounced?

(16) e.g.   I **use**dt'live in Ibaraki Prefecture.
I didn't **use**t'like natto.

Exercise 2

Write one sentence each using *used to* and *didn't use to* about your junior high school days.   あなたの中学生時代についてused toとdidn't use toを用いた文を1つずつ書きなさい。

1. _____

2. _____

Now tell your partner about your personality and situation at junior high school, taking care of the pronunciation.

📖 **Language Note**

When discussing likes and dislikes, use gerunds with these verbs: *enjoy, dislike, don't mind, can't stand*; and gerunds or infinitives with these verbs: *like, love, hate*.

e.g.	I enjoy watching sports. ✓	I love watching sports. ✓
	I enjoy to watch sports. ✕	I love to watch sports. ✓

好き嫌いについて述べる時、*enjoy, dislike, don't mind, can't stand*のような動詞の後ろには動名詞を用いますが、*like, love, hate*のような動詞には動名詞、不定詞のどちらでもかまいません。

Warm-up
Unit 1
Unit 2
Unit 3
Review 1
Unit 4
Unit 5
Unit 6
Review 2

❸ Model Conversation

Exercise 1

Todd is talking to Hiro about his junior high school life.

Listen and read the conversation. Then practice the conversation with your partner.

Model Conversation

Todd: I didn't know you ①did kendo.

Hiro : Yes, I used to belong to the ②kendo club.

Todd: I wasn't very ③athletic at junior high. I couldn't stand ④playing sports.

Hiro : Really? I used to love ⑤all sports.

Exercise 2

Substitute the underlined parts in the model. Start by reading the conversation directly and substituting. Try to only look at the substitution part by the last time.

A	B	C
① could draw	① played the trumpet	① were good at chess
② anime	② brass band	② board game
③ creative	③ musical	③ competitive
④ art class	④ music class	④ games
⑤ making things	⑤ that class the most	⑤ beating my friends

❹ Grammar Exercises

Exercise 1

Using *use/d to*, write a suitable verb (with extra words if necessary) in the space to complete the sentences.

1. I _____ baseball, but now I prefer soccer.

2. She _____, but she got divorced last year.

3. Yumi _____, but she quit when she entered university.

4. Did you _____ in Tokyo?

5. When they were high school students, they _____ after school.

6. John didn't _____ well, but now he is very good.

7. _____ a DVD rental store near my house, but it closed down last year.

8. In the Edo Period in Japan, people _____ .

9. Keisuke is too busy now, but he often _____ in his free time.

10. Didn't you _____ glasses?

Exercise **2**

Circle the correct word to complete the sentences in the story. (If both verb forms are possible, circle both.)

> Last weekend I (went / used to go) to the movie theater with my friend for the first time in a year. I often (went / used to go) to the movie theater before I (got / used to get) my part-time job, but recently I have been busy and haven't had time.
>
> We (watched / used to watch) a historical drama about a samurai warrior who (lived / used to live) in Shikoku during the Edo period. In the movie the warrior (went / used to go) to Kyushu to fight in a famous battle. He (won / used to win) the battle, but was injured and was killed at the end of the movie.
>
> It (was / used to be) a very good movie, and my friend (liked / used to like) it too because he (lived / used to live) in Shikoku during his elementary school days.

Exercise **3**

Complete the following to make *true* sentences about you.

1. I used to _____ , but I quit.

2. When I was _____ , I used to _____ .

3. I never used to be able to _____ .

4. I used to like _____ , but now I prefer _____ .

5. My (_____) used to _____ .

⑤ **Pair Dictation**

Student A: Turn to page 95.   **Student B: Turn to page 105.**

❶ Vocabulary review

| Exercise 1 ————————————————————

(18) Yudai is talking to his grandfather about life during the bubble period.
Which does his grandfather prefer: life now or during the bubble?

————————————————————

| Exercise 2 ————————————————————

Listen again and make notes about the differences between the bubble period and
the present day.

Bubble Period	Present Day

| Exercise 3 ————————————————————

Write three true sentences each about both periods.

Bubble period

1. _____

2. _____

3. _____

Present day

1. _____

2. _____

3. _____

❷ Personalized Conversation

Exercise 1

Two years ago John's doctor told him to change his lifestyle.

Look at the two pictures. How has John changed? With your partner, can you find seven lifestyle changes?

ジョンを診ている医師が、ライフスタイルを変えるようにと2年前に言いました。2枚の絵を見て、ジョンがどのように変わったかをパートナーと観察しなさい。7つの変化を見つけることができますか。

Student A: Turn to page 96.（see picture A）
Student B: Turn to page 106.（see picture B）

Exercise 2

Now write seven sentences describing these life style changes.

1. _____

2. _____

3. _____

4. _____

5. _____

6. _____

7. _____

Exercise 3

Do you have a healthy lifestyle? What could you do to improve your health?
Write five sentences.

e.g.   I should exercise more.   I could start going to the gym.

1. _____

2. _____

3. _____

4. _____

5. _____

Exercise 4

Tell a new partner about how you could improve your health.

❸ Listening: Model Speech

(19) Listen and read Mai's speech about her elementary school days.

(Model Speech)

My Elementary School Days

I entered my local elementary school in the spring of 2010 when I was six years old. I was very excited and I entered with some of my friends from kindergarten, so I wasn't so nervous. The elementary school was near my house, so every day I used to walk to school with students from the same apartment building as me. When I was 11 years old, I became the leader of the group and had to guide the younger students.

I was at elementary school for six years, from 2010 to 2016. We studied many different subjects and had to do homework, but of course, it was easier than junior high or high school. My favorite subject was social studies. We also played many sports in P.E. and, once a year, we had a sports day, which was a lot of fun.

I had many good friends at school and, on the way home after school, we often used to play in the local park near the school. We graduated from elementary school in March, 2016 and some of my friends entered different junior high schools, but I still meet them sometimes and we talk about our happy school days.

4 Personalized Speech

Write a speech about your elementary school days.

Warm-up

Unit 1

Unit 2

Unit 3

Review 1

Unit 4

Unit 5

Unit 6

Review 2

⑤ Speech: Pair Discussion

Exercise 1

Now work in pairs. Read your speech to your conversation partner. Listen carefully to your partner's speech.

Exercise 2

Ask your partner questions. First, write 3 follow-up questions.

> Examples of questions:
> What was your favorite subject at elementary school?
> Who was your favorite teacher?
> How long did it take to walk to school from your house?

MY QUESTIONS

1. _____ ?
2. _____ ?
3. _____ ?

Exercise 3

Now ask your questions.

Exercise 4

Take two minutes to memorize your speech. Then, close the textbook and try to make the speech again. (It is not important to repeat your speech perfectly, just try to remember as much as you can!)

1

❶Interview Test Questions

Answer the questions about yourself with complete sentences.

次の質問に主語・述語のある完全な英文で答えなさい。

 1. What would your ideal life be?

_____

2. What would you do if you had a lot of money?

_____

3. Would you like to get married and have children in the future?

_____

4. If you had more free time, how would you use it?

_____

5. What would you do if you felt sick in class?

_____

6. If your friend had a fever, what advice would you give them?

_____

7. Are you worrying about anything these days?

_____

8. Do you want to quit anything?

_____

9. When you were in elementary school, what were you like?

_____

10. Did you use to belong to a club at junior high?

_____

11. What was your favorite subject at elementary school?

_____

12. Is there anything you would like to change about yourself?

_____

Grammar

Circle the correct word(s).

1. If you _____ down this street, you will see the park on the left.
   [go / went / gone]

2. When I was a child, I used to _____ dodgeball.
   [play / played / playing]

3. _____ smoke. It's bad for your health.
   [You should / How about / Don't]

4. If I _____ an animal, I'd like to be a dog.
   [am / was / were]

5. I used to _____ run very fast.
   [can / be able to / could]

6. _____ watching a movie?
   [How about / Would you / Why don't you]

7. If you were rich, what _____ do?
   [will you / would you / do you]

8. Did you _____ English when you were a child?
   [studied / use to study / studying]

9. If I _____ you, I'd study harder.
   [am / are / were]

10. _____ you hurry, you won't catch the bus. It's too late.
    [Even / Even if / Even as]

◆3▸ Vocabulary

Write the words below in the correct spaces.

creative	fever	graduation	lottery	medicine
outgoing	overweight	stomachache	temperature	toothache

1. I got some _____ from the doctor for my _____.

2. She is very _____. She loves drawing and writing stories.

3. I'm looking forward to the _____ ceremony.

4. He's a little _____. He should exercise more.

5. John is very _____. He loves meeting and talking to people.

6. If you have a _____, you should go to the dentist.

7. I bought a _____ ticket. I hope I win!

8. His _____ is very high. I think he has a _____.

Warm-up

Unit 1

Unit 2

Unit 3

Review 1

Unit 4

Unit 5

Unit 6

Review 2

④ Writing I

Put the sentences in the correct order.

1. a teacher / be / used to / she

_____.

2. the park / you / don't / to / go / why

_____?

3. university / graduate / will / you / when / from

_____?

4. be / to / like / the future / successful / in / I'd

_____.

5. class / you / sleep / in / shouldn't

_____.

6. you / if / I / I'd / hard / study / were

_____.

7. Starbucks / going / about / how / to

_____?

8. use to / hair / long / did / have / you

_____?

9. very / I / I / was / was / a child / shy / when

_____.

10. if / lost / you / you / would / wallet / your / what / do

_____?

◆⑤ Writing II

Write a question *or* sentence (A) to match the reply (B). (There may be more than one correct sentence or question.)

1. A: _____ ?

B: Fine, thanks. How about you?

2. A: _____ ?

B: In the future? I want to be a businessman.

3. A: _____ .

B: Then you should go to the dentist.

4. A: _____ ?

B: The lottery? I'd probably buy a nice car.

5. A: _____ ?

B: My favorite subject was social studies.

6. A: _____ ?

B: Yes. I'd like to have one boy and one girl.

7. A: _____ ?

B: No. I've always had short hair.

8. A: _____ .

B: Why don't you take some medicine?

9. A: _____ ?

B: Yes. I lived in Tokyo for three years.

10. A: _____ !

B: Congratulations!

⑥ Comprehension

Read Tomoki's letter to his future self. Answer the questions with complete sentences.

To be opened on July 5th, 2040

Dear Future Me,

❖ How are you? Are you fine? Did your dreams come true? I hope so. When you were younger, you were very ambitious. You said you would move to New York and work for an international company by the time you were thirty. You thought you would quit that job and start your own business. You used to work hard at university and also study English in your free time. Can you speak English fluently now?

❖ Did you get married? How is your family life? You always imagined you would marry your college girlfriend and have two children—a boy and a girl. You used to enjoy watching American movies on weekends and wanted to live in an apartment near Central Park. You imagined eating hot dogs in the park with your family like in the movies!

❖ If you could change anything about your life now, what would it be?

Take care,

Tomoki (21 years old)

1. What does Tomoki hope about his future self?

_____

2. What was he like when he was younger?

_____

3. When did he plan to move to New York?

_____

4. After working for an international company, what did Tomoki plan to do?

_____

5. What did he use to do in his free time at university?

_____

6. Who did he think he would marry?

_____

7. How many children did he want to have?

_____

8. What did he enjoy doing on weekends?

_____

9. Why did he imagine eating hot dogs in Central Park?

_____

10. Are you like Tomoki? Why or why not?

_____

Warm-up

Unit 1

Unit 2

Unit 3

Review 1

Unit 4

Unit 5

Unit 6

Review 2

When was this building designed?

Part **A**

1 Warm Up: Key Vocabulary

Exercise **1**

Label the activities with words from the box.

1. write a book ( )	**7.** make a model ( )
2. create a sculpture ( )	**8.** sing a song ( )
3. direct a movie ( )	**9.** design a building ( )
4. produce a record ( )	**10.** build a bridge ( )
5. film a movie ( )	**11.** found a company ( )
6. paint a picture ( )	

a.

b.

c.

d.

e.

f.

g. h. i.

j. k.

Exercise 2

Write the simple past passive form next to the plain form.

create	was created	paint	_____
direct	_____	produce	_____
film	_____	sing	_____
make	_____	write	_____
design	_____	build	_____
found	_____		

Exercise 3

Think of your favorite movie, song, or book. Look at the example, then write three sentences describing it. Try to use the simple past passive form once if you can.

好きな映画・歌・本のことを考えなさい。例にならって、それについて3つの文を書きなさい。1つは受動態の過去形にしなさい。

Hint   Simple past: John Lennon *wrote* the song "Yesterday."

         Simple past passive: The song "Yesterday" *was written by* John Lennon.

e.g.   1. My favorite book is "Harry Potter and the Philosopher's Stone."

        2. It was written by J. K. Rowling.

        3. I like it because the story is so exciting.

1. _____

2. _____

3. _____

Exercise 4

Tell your partner about your favorites. After you listen to your partner's favorites, try to think of a follow-up question for each favorite.

❷ Pronunciation

| Exercise 1

(23) Listen to the following sentences and add stress marks (ʹ) to the stressed words.

次の文を聞いて、強く発音される語にアクセント符号（ʹ）をつけなさい。

1. I'm glad you like it.

2. I've never heard of her.

3. What do you think of it?

4. Have you met him?

5. Do you know them?

What types of words are stressed? Discuss with a partner.

| Exercise 2

Using "Read, Remember, Repeat," take turns reading the sentences in Pronunciation Exercise 1 with your partner. Can you input the correct stress pattern?

📖 Language Note

Typically, subject pronouns (I, you, he, she, it, they) and object pronouns (me. you, him, her, it, them) are functional words in sentences, so are not stressed. Content words (verbs, nouns, etc.) are usually stressed.

概して、主語になる代名詞（I, you, he, she, it, theyなど）や目的語になる代名詞（me, you, him, her, it, themなど）は機能語であるために、アクセントは置かれない。内容語（動詞、名詞など）は通常、アクセントが置かれる。

❸ Model Conversation

| Exercise 1 ────────────────────

(24) **Rena is talking to Martin about the song they are listening to.**
Listen and read the conversation. Then practice the conversation with your partner.

Model Conversation

Rena　：　Who ①wrote this ②song?

Martin：　Oh, it was ③written by ④One Direction.
　　　　　Do you know *them*?

Rena　：　No, I don't. But the ②song is really good.

Martin：　I'm glad you like it.

| Exercise 2 ────────────────────

Substitute the underlined parts in the model conversation and change the *italic* part where necessary. Start by reading the conversation directly and substituting. Try to only look at the substitution part by the last time. イタリック体のthemを必要に応じて変えなさい。

A	B	C
① made	① directed	① painted
② lasagna	② movie	② picture
③ made	③ directed	③ painted
④ Arisa [f.]	④ Quentin Tarantino [m.]	④ Yayoi Kusama [f.]

4 Grammar Exercises

Exercise **1**

Match the verb from the box to the correct sentence and put into the passive form.
Remember to use the correct tense (*is/are* or *was/were*).

ask	cancel	damage	injure	invite	know
paint	sell	speak	steal		

1. Maria _____ to her friend's birthday party last week.

2. The teacher is sick today, so the class _____.

3. My house _____ in the typhoon.

4. I _____ to work overtime by my boss last night.

5. Kyoto _____ for its beautiful temples and shrines.

6. Spanish is an international language. It _____ in about 20 countries.

7. Some people _____ in the accident.

8. Japanese cars _____ all over the world.

9. He called the police because his bike _____.

10. The Mona Lisa _____ by Leonardo da Vinci.

Exercise 2

Add the correct verb from the list in the following passage. Remember to include *is / are* or *was / were*.

次の文の空欄に下の動詞から適したものを選び、受動態にして文を完成しなさい。*is / are* や *was / were* を忘れないようにしましょう。

enjoy	make	publish	release	translate	write

J. K. Rowling and Harry Potter

Have you ever heard of Harry Potter? He is a very famous book and movie character. The *Harry Potter* novels _____ by J. K. Rowling. The first *Harry Potter* book _____ in 1997 and soon became popular all over the world. Her books _____ into many languages, including Japanese.

After a few years, the *Harry Potter* books _____ into movies. The first *Harry Potter* movie _____ in 2001 and was a huge hit in many countries. *Harry Potter* books and movies are still very popular and _____ by both adults and children.

J. K. Rowling

Exercise 3

Change the following into passive sentences.

e.g.   Many people watched the movie.
         The movie was watched by many people.

1. Steve Jobs invented the iPhone.

_____.

2. The police arrested a young man.

_____.

3. Columbus discovered the continent of America.

_____.

4. I drew this picture.

_____.

5. My brother gave a present to me.

_____.

⑤ Pair Dictation

Student A: Turn to page 98.   **Student B: Turn to page 108.**

❶ Vocabulary Review

Exercise **1**

(25) **Miyu is visiting the Guggenheim Art Museum in New York.**
Listen to the guide explain about the artworks and match the name of the work
with the person who made it and the year it was made.

ミユはニューヨークのグッゲンハイム美術館に来ています。

ガイドの説明を聞いて、作品名、製作者の名前、製作年を結びつけましょう。

Artwork's name	Creator's name	Year
1. *Woman with Yellow Hair* ·	· Henry Moore ·	· 1931
2. *Three Standing Figures* ·	· Frank Lloyd Wright ·	· 1943
3. Mural ·	· Pablo Picasso ·	· 1947
4. Guggenheim Museum ·	· Jackson Pollock ·	· 1956

Exercise **2**

Listen again. What is Miyu's opinion on each piece?

1. *Woman with Yellow Hair* _____

2. *Three Standing Figures* _____

3. Mural _____

4. Guggenheim Museum _____

Exercise **3**

Write complete sentences about each artwork in Exercise 1.

1. _____

2. _____

3. _____

4. _____

Exercise 4

Is there an art museum you would like to visit? Where is it and why do you want to go there?

_____

_____

2 Personalized Conversation

Exercise 1

Change the following statements to Were you ...? or Have you ...? opening questions. Then think of a suitable follow-up question.

Opening Questionの欄にある語句をWere you ...?かHave you ...?で始まる文に変えなさい。つぎに、それに関連する質問を考えて、**Follow-up Question**の欄に書きましょう。

e.g.　Opening question: Were you woken up by an alarm clock this morning?
　　　Follow-up question: What time did you get up?

Find someone who:		
Opening Question	Follow-up Question	Name
1. was woken up by an alarm clock this morning.	Q: _____ ? A: _____	
2. has been bitten by a dog.	Q: _____ ? A: _____	
3. was helped by someone recently.	Q: _____ ? A: _____	
4. has been injured in an accident	Q: _____ ? A: _____	
5. was taken out for dinner recently.	Q: _____ ? A: _____	
6. was given a gift recently.	Q: _____ ? A: _____	

（次ページへつづく）

7. was taken ill recently.	Q: _____ ?		
	A: _____		
8. was invited to a party recently.	Q: _____ ?		
	A: _____		
9. has been told off by a teacher recently.	Q: _____ ?		
	A: _____		
10. was asked to do something today.	Q: _____ ?		
	A: _____		

Exercise 2

Find out what your classmates have experienced. 次のルールに従ってクラスメートがどんなことを経験したか見つけなさい。

Rules: You can only write a student who answers, "yes" to the first question.

You can only write a student's name once.

You must form a pair and ask each other, not in a group.

Hints: You should only use English, so use **"Key Point Shadowing"** and **Classroom English** to help you communicate.

ルール：最初の質問に「はい」と答えた学生の名前をNameの欄に書くことができます。

1人の学生の名前は1回のみ記入できます。

グループではなく、ペアーを組んで質問し合いなさい。

ヒント：英語のみを使用します。困った時には、"Key Point Shadowing"やClassroom Englishを使用しましょう。

Exercise 3

Tell your partner the most interesting thing you found out.

❸ Listening: Model Speech

(26) **Listen to Shuya talk about his favorite movie *Star Wars*.**

Model Speech

My Favorite Movie: *Star Wars*

Do you know *Star Wars*? My favorite movies are the *Star Wars* movies. They are a series of science fiction or space fantasy movies and are set in a galaxy far away. The first *Star Wars* movie was released in 1977, a long time before I was born. It was directed by George Lucas. Each *Star Wars* movie has a separate story, but the stories are all connected and some of them have the same characters. Actually the first *Star Wars* movie is the fourth story in the series. (It's a little complicated!) There are now nine main *Star Wars* movies, in addition to some other related movies.

These movies are loved by people all over the world. I have all of these movies on DVD and have watched them many times. Why do I like *Star Wars* so much? There are many reasons. The stories are interesting, the action scenes are very exciting and the special effects are excellent. Also, there are many fascinating characters. My favorite character is Luke Skywalker, who is played by the actor Mark Hamil.

If another *Star Wars* movie is released in the future, I will definitely watch it.

Warm-up
Unit 1
Unit 2
Unit 3
Review 1
Unit 4
Unit 5
Unit 6
Review 2

 **Personalized Speech**

Write a speech about your favorite movie, TV series or book(s).

What is it about? Who was it written/directed by? Why do you like it?

⑤ Speech: Pair Discussion

Exercise 1

Now work in pairs. Read your speech to your conversation partner. Listen carefully to your partner's speech.

Exercise 2

Ask your partner questions. First, write 3 follow-up questions.

> Examples of questions:
> When did you first read/see it?
> Which movie/book/episode did you like best?
> How many times have you watched/read it.

MY QUESTIONS

1. _____ ?
2. _____ ?
3. _____ ?

Exercise 3

Now ask your questions.

Exercise 4

Take two minutes to memorize your speech. Then, close the textbook and try to make the speech again. (It is not important to repeat your speech perfectly, just try to remember as much as you can!)

Where is your hometown located?

❶ Warm Up: Key Vocabulary

| Exercise **1**

Match the adjective to the picture.

1. boring	( )	**6.** historic	( )	**10.** polluted	( )
2. crowded	( )	**7.** cosmopolitan	( )	**11.** peaceful	( )
3. lively	( )	**8.** touristy	( )	**12.** remote	( )
4. ugly	( )	**9.** unique	( )	**13.** picturesque	( )
5. industrial	( )				

a.

b.

c.

d.

e.

f.

g.

h.

i.

j.

k.

l.

m.

Exercise 2

With a partner, decide whether these are positive attributes, negative attributes, or could be considered either. Fill in the table below.

Exercise 1 の形容詞は、肯定的・否定的どちらのニュアンスがあるか、あるいはどちらにもなりうるかを、パートナーと相談して決めなさい。

Positive (＋)	Negative (－)	Either (＋, －)

Exercise 3

Which of these adjectives describe where you come from? Write two sentences describing your hometown.

1. _____

2. _____

Exercise 4

Read your sentences to a partner. Can you think of an appropriate follow-up question?

❷ Pronunciation

Exercise 1

(28) **Listen to how the adjectives are pronounced. How many syllables can you count?**

Adjective	Number of syllables	Most stressed syllable	Adjective	Number of syllables	Most stressed syllable
boring crowded lively ugly industrial historic cosmopolitan	2	1st	touristy unique polluted peaceful remote picturesque		

Exercise 2

Listen again. Which syllable has the most stress?

Exercise 3

Take turns practicing reading the adjectives. Be careful placing the stress on the correct syllable.

Exercise 4

Change partners. Using what you have learned, tell each other about where you come from (Warm-up Exercise 3).

③ Model Conversation

Exercise 1

(29) **Andrew and Nana are talking about where they are from.**
Listen and read the conversation. Then practice the conversation with your partner.

> Model Conversation
>
> Andrew: I'm from a ①place called ②Liverpool.
>
> It's ③famous for the Beatles.
>
> Nana : So, what's it like living there?
>
> Andrew: Well, it's ④cosmopolitan, *but* ⑤crowded.
>
> But I like it!
>
> Nana : I'd like to visit one day.
>
> Andrew: Sure, anytime.

Exercise 2

Substitute the underlined parts in the model and change the *italic* part where necessary. Start by reading the conversation directly and substituting. Try to only look at the substitution part by the last time.

A	B	C
① town	① city in England	① region in France
② Yokkaichi	② Oxford	② Burgundy
③ located in Mie Prefecture	③ known for its university	③ famous for its wine
④ industrial	④ historic	④ peaceful
⑤ polluted	⑤ touristy	⑤ remote

◆4 Grammar Exercises

Exercise 1

Circle the correct form of the adjective.

1. Who is the [more famous / most famous] athlete in Japan?

2. The USA has more people but Canada is [bigger / biggest].

3. Where is the [nearer / nearest] ATM?

4. Which is [more popular / most popular] in Japan, soccer or baseball?

5. She is not the [taller / tallest] person in her class, but she's the best basketball player.

6. There are four main islands in Japan, and Honshu is [the bigger / the biggest].

7. Do you think Chinese is [more difficult / most difficult] than English?

8. I like Kyoto more than Tokyo. It's [more historic / most historic].

9. Disneyland is maybe the [more crowded / most crowded] place I've ever been to.

10. My father is 188 centimeters tall, but my brother is even [taller / tallest]!

Exercise **2**

Circle the correct verb form in the sentences. If both are correct, circle BOTH of them.

1. She enjoys *to meet / meeting* her friends on the weekend.

2. Alan likes *to play / playing* baseball, but he prefers *to watch / watching* soccer.

3. Do you want *to go / going* out tonight?

4. I don't mind *to work / working* on weekends, but I really don't want *to work / working* next Saturday. I would like *to take / taking* a break.

5. How about *to watch / watching* a movie tomorrow? I'd like *to see / seeing* the new Conan movie.

6. Mary started *to work / working* as a nurse last year.

7. Turn left at the next corner and keep *to go / going* straight.

8. Mr. Itoh was worried about his health, so he quit *to smoke / smoking* last year.

9. Oh no! I forgot *to do / doing* my homework!

10. The new students dislike *to study / studying* online every day. They want *to go / going* to campus *to meet / meeting* their friends.

11. Would you like anything *to drink / drinking* with your meal?

12. Miya decided *to quit / quitting* the tennis club after the summer.

13. I've never been abroad, so I'd like *to go / going* somewhere soon, maybe Canada.

14. Please stay! I don't want you *to go / going* yet.

⑤ **Pair Dictation**

Student A: Turn to page 99.   **Student B: Turn to page 109.**

❶ Vocabulary Review

│Exercise 1 ———————————————————

Taiki and Asuka are discussing where they are from in an English class at a university in Nagoya. Listen to the conversation and write down where they are from.

Asuka: _____	Taiki: _____

│Exercise 2 ———————————————————

Listen again and write notes describing what they say about each place.

│Exercise 3 ———————————————————

Write two sentences each about each place.

Asuka:

1. _____

2. _____

Taiki:

1. _____

2. _____

Compare your sentences with a partner.

⑤ Speech: Pair Discussion

Exercise 1

Now work in pairs. Read your speech to your conversation partner. Listen carefully to your partner's speech.

Exercise 2

Ask your partner questions. First, write 3 follow-up questions.

> Examples of questions:
> When did you first read/see it?
> Which movie/book/episode did you like best?
> How many times have you watched/read it.

MY QUESTIONS

1. _____ ?

2. _____ ?

3. _____ ?

Exercise 3

Now ask your questions.

Exercise 4

Take two minutes to memorize your speech. Then, close the textbook and try to make the speech again. (It is not important to repeat your speech perfectly, just try to remember as much as you can!)

Where is your hometown located?

1 Warm Up: Key Vocabulary

Exercise 1

Match the adjective to the picture.

1. boring ( )	**6.** historic ( )	**10.** polluted ( )
2. crowded ( )	**7.** cosmopolitan ( )	**11.** peaceful ( )
3. lively ( )	**8.** touristy ( )	**12.** remote ( )
4. ugly ( )	**9.** unique ( )	**13.** picturesque ( )
5. industrial ( )		

a.

b.

c.

d.

e.

f.

g.

h.

i.

j.

k.

l.

m.

Exercise 2

With a partner, decide whether these are positive attributes, negative attributes, or could be considered either. Fill in the table below.

Exercise 1の形容詞は、肯定的・否定的どちらのニュアンスがあるか、あるいはどちらにもなりうるかを、パートナーと相談して決めなさい。

Positive（＋）	Negative（－）	Either（＋，－）

Exercise 3

Which of these adjectives describe where you come from? Write two sentences describing your hometown.

1. _____

2. _____

Exercise 4

Read your sentences to a partner. Can you think of an appropriate follow-up question?

② Pronunciation

Exercise 1

(28) Listen to how the adjectives are pronounced. How many syllables can you count?

Adjective	Number of syllables	Most stressed syllable	Adjective	Number of syllables	Most stressed syllable
boring	2	1st	touristy		
crowded			unique		
lively			polluted		
ugly			peaceful		
industrial			remote		
historic			picturesque		
cosmopolitan					

Exercise 2

Listen again. Which syllable has the most stress?

Exercise 3

Take turns practicing reading the adjectives. Be careful placing the stress on the correct syllable.

Exercise 4

Change partners. Using what you have learned, tell each other about where you come from (Warm-up Exercise 3).

Exercise 4

Which place would you prefer to live in, and why?

❷ Personalized Conversation

Exercise 1

With a partner, try to think of questions to find out the following information about a city.

1. Location:　Where is Tokyo located ?

2. Population:

3. Weather:

4. Industry:

5. Nickname:

Exercise 2&3

Change partners.

Student A: Turn to page 100.　　　Student B: Turn to page 110.

③ Listening: Model Speech

 Listen to Rinka talk about Kagoshima.

Model Speech

Welcome to Kagoshima City

Do you know Kagoshima? It is a prefecture in the southern island of Kyushu, and Kagoshima City is the prefectural capital. It is located in the south of Kyushu and the population of Kagoshima City is about 600,000.

Kagoshima City is most famous for Sakurajima, which is a large picturesque volcano that can be seen from the city. It is an active volcano that sometimes erupts and often blows ash over the city. I think it is unique. Kagoshima is also a very historic place and used to be called *Satsuma*. It is famous for the samurai Saigo Takamori, who led a rebellion in 1877, and there are some interesting museums in the city.

Although it is a little industrial, more and more people are visiting Kagoshima these days, and it is becoming more touristy. There is a lively downtown area that has many places to eat and drink. The food is great and Kagoshima is famous for its *shochu,* which is a kind of alcoholic drink made from sweet potatoes.

You can get to Kagoshima by plane, by *Shinkansen* or local trains. There is even a ferry to Okinawa. I hope you will visit there someday.

④ Personalized Speech

Write a speech about a place (city, prefecture, area) you like or know in Japan.
(This is probably a place you have been to.)

_____

_____

_____

_____

_____

⑤ Speech: Pair Discussion

| Exercise 1

Now work in pairs. Read your speech to your conversation partner. Listen carefully to your partner's speech.

| Exercise 2

Ask your partner questions. First, write 3 follow-up questions.

> Examples of questions:
> When did you first go there?
> What is the best time of the year to visit?
> How many times have you been there?

MY QUESTIONS

1. _____ ?

2. _____ ?

3. _____ ?

| Exercise 3

Now ask your questions.

| Exercise 4

Take two minutes to memorize your speech. Then, close the textbook and try to make the speech again. (It is not important to repeat your speech perfectly, just try to remember as much as you can!)

Did you clean up your room?

❶ Warm Up: Key Vocabulary

| Exercise 1

Phrasal verbs are made up of verbs and adverbs. 句動詞は動詞と副詞から成り立っています。

Choose the adverbs from the box to complete the phrasal verbs. Some adverbs may be used more than once.

away / in /off / on / out / up

put _____ *your* shoes

put _____ decorations

put _____ the dishes

take _____ *your* shoes

switch _____ the light

switch _____ the light

hang _____ *your* clothes   hang _____ the futon   clean _____ *your* room

bring _____ the washing   throw _____ the trash

Exercise 2

Write three Japanese rules or customs for polite living.

Hint: Use *should/have to + phrasal verb + before/after + gerund*

e.g.   You should clean up your room before going to bed.
       People have to switch off the light after leaving a room.

1. _____

2. _____

3. _____

Exercise 3

Compare your rules and customs with your partner. Are there any you disagree on?

② Pronunciation

Exercise 1

When phrasal verbs are used as verbs, the adverb is stressed, not the verb.
句動詞の場合、動詞ではなく副詞にアクセントが置かれます。

Predict the correct stress patterns for the following sentences by writing a ✓ in the ( ).

33	1. Cán you bríng in the wáshing? ( )	Can you bring ín the wáshing? ( )
	2. Alwáys táke óff your shóes. ( )	Alwáys take óff your shóes. ( )
	3. Pléase throw awáy the trásh. ( )	Please throw awáy the trásh. ( )
	4. Try tó clean up yóur róom today. ( )	Trý to clean úp your róom todáy. ( )
	5. Remémber to switch óff the líght. ( )	Remember tó switch óff the líght. ( )

Exercise 2

Now listen and check your predictions. Then take turns practicing reading the sentences with the correct stress patterns.

③ Model Conversation

Exercise 1

34 **Fred, an international exchange student, is talking to his host mother. Listen and read the conversation. Then practice the conversation with your partner.**

		Model Conversation
Fred	:	Are there any ①house rules?
Host mother:		Yes, be sure to ②say *itadakimasu* before ③starting your meal.
Fred	:	Yes, I heard Japanese ④families always do that.
Host mother:		And try to ⑤tidy up your room if you can.
Fred	:	Okay. I'll try to remember.

Exercise 2

Substitute the underlined parts in the model conversation. Start by reading the conversation directly and substituting. Try to only look at the substitution part by the last time.

A	B	C
① dorm	① school	① company
② wash your body	② take off your shoes	② take part in *rajio taiso*
③ entering the bath	③ entering the school building	③ starting work
④ people	④ students	④ employees
⑤ be back by 11:00p.m.	⑤ greet every teacher	⑤ finish your work on time

4 Grammar Exercises

Exercise 1

A. Complete the following sentences with *which, who, where* or *when*.

1. Kyoto is a city _____ there are many famous temples.

2. Christmas in America is a time _____ people exchange presents and people _____ are Christian go to church.

3. Starbucks is a coffee shop chain _____ has many branches all over the world.

4. O-Bon is a special holiday in the summer _____ many people in Japan return to the place _____ they were born.

5. *Frozen* is a Disney movie _____ she has seen over ten times.

6. Karate is a martial art from Japan _____ has spread around the world.

B. Write *true* sentences with the relatives.

1. I like people who _____.

2. _____ is a famous company that sells _____.

3. I want to go somewhere where _____.

4. _____ is a season when _____ .

5. _____ Prefecture is a place where _____ .

6. _____ is/was a famous _____ who

_____ .

7. English is a language that _____ .

Exercise 2

Sometimes in English the object of the sentence is in the MIDDLE of a phrasal verb. Complete the sentences with a phrasal verb.

句動詞を使用する時、目的語が動詞と副詞の間に置かれることがあります。例に従って、下の空所に適する句動詞を入れて文を完成しなさい。

e.g.　It's cold outside. I'm going to *put* my coat *on*.

1. Here's the entrance. Don't forget to _____ your shoes _____ .

2. I'm going to _____ this picture _____ on the wall here.

3. _____ the music _____ , please! It's noisy!

4. I _____ the garbage _____ in front of my apartment every Monday morning.

5. The battery is dead. I can't _____ my phone _____ .

6. Where can I _____ my coat _____ ?

7. Do you _____ decorations _____ for Christmas?

8. Please _____ your garbage _____ after the barbecue.

9. Your room is messy. You should _____ it _____ .

10. It's raining. Can you _____ the washing _____ , please?

⑤ Pair Dictation

Student A: Turn to page 101.　　　**Student B: Turn to page 111.**

① Vocabulary Review

Exercise 1

(35) Anna is talking to Yui, a Japanese exchange student living in the U.S., about a future trip to Kyoto.

Listen to the dialog. What does Yui recommend Anna should do? What does she recommend she shouldn't do? Write in the numbered sections in the table below.

Should	Should not
1)	1)
2)	2)
3)	3)
4)	

Exercise 2

Listen to the dialog again. Add any extra information Yui includes about the advice in space provided.

Exercise 3

What would you recommend a foreign tourist do or not do in Kyoto?

Should   Should not

_____   _____

_____   _____

_____   _____

Now compare with a partner.

❷ Personalized Conversation

Exercise 1

Look at the picture of a foreign student staying in a dormitory in Japan. With a partner write a list of 8 rules to post on the noticeboard.

Hint: Use   *Always ~*   *Try to ~*
                 Never ~   *Remember to ~*
                 Don't ~   *before/after ~ing*

Dorm Rules

1. _____

2. _____

3. _____

4. _____

5. _____

6. _____

7. _____

8. _____

Exercise 2

Compare your rules with another pair of students. Do you find any differences?

Warm-up
Unit 1
Unit 2
Unit 3
Review 1
Unit 4
Unit 5
Unit 6
Review 2

❸ Listening: Model Speech

 Listen to Kota talk about New Year in Japan.

(Model Speech)

New Year in Japan

As in many countries, New Year is a very important time in Japan. At the end of the year, most people are very busy, but many companies have end-of-year parties for their workers. These are called *bonenkai* in Japanese. Although you can see many Christmas decorations at this time, Christmas Day is not a national holiday in Japan. Before New Year, it is also important to write special New Year's cards (*nengajo*), which are delivered on New Year's Day. Most families return to their hometown for New Year's Eve. Before midnight many people eat a special dish of buckwheat noodles called *toshikoshi soba* and watch the famous music program called the *Kohaku,* which is broadcast every year and watched by millions of people.

On New Year's Day, or in the first few days of the year, it is a custom to visit a shrine or temple to pray for good fortune for the coming year. This first visit is called *hatsumode.* Back at home many people eat a traditional New Year dish called *osechi ryori* and relax with their family. Of course, New Year's Day is a national holiday, and most people have a three-day holiday before going back to work.

Although recently more and more young people gather for a New Year countdown on New Year's Eve, the traditional New Year in Japan is rather quiet.

❹ Personalized Speech

Write a speech about a festival, holiday, or custom in Japan. You can write about a local festival or a national event.

Warm-up

Unit 1

Unit 2

Unit 3

Review 1

Unit 4

Unit 5

Unit 6

Review 2

⑤ Speech: Pair Discussion

Exercise 1

Now work in pairs. Read your speech to your conversation partner. Listen
carefully to your partner's speech.

Exercise 2

Ask your partner questions. First, write 3 follow-up questions.

> Examples of questions:
>
> How many times have you been to/participated in _____ ?
>
> Is there some special food for this?
>
> Will you _____ next time?

MY QUESTIONS

1. _____ ?
2. _____ ?
3. _____ ?

Exercise 3

Now ask your questions.

Exercise 4

Take two minutes to memorize your speech. Then, close the textbook and try to
make the speech again. (It is not important to repeat your speech perfectly, just
try to remember as much as you can!)

◆1 Interview Test Questions

Answer the questions about yourself with complete sentences.

1. Have you ever been injured?

_____

2. Were you taken to the hospital?

_____

3. How many times have you been on a school trip?

_____

4. Which school trip did you like best?

_____

5. What is the best place you have ever visited?

_____

6. When is the best time to visit there?

_____

7. What is it like living in your hometown?

_____

8. What is it known for?

_____

9. Does your school have many rules?

_____

10. Which rule do you like least?

_____

11. What customs are there in Japan?

_____

12. Are there any customs that foreign people do not understand?

_____

Warm-up

Unit 1

Unit 2

Unit 3

Review 1

Unit 4

Unit 5

Unit 6

Review 2

❷ Grammar

Circle the correct word(s).

1. If I had more money, I _____ go abroad.
　　[will / would / am going to]

2. I used to _____ play tennis well, but I haven't played for a long time.
　　[be able to / can / could]

3. What would you do if you _____ your smartphone?
　　[lose / losing / lost]

4. The next movie will _____ in December.
　　[release / be released / be releasing]

5. YouTube is the website _____ I use most.
　　[when / that / where]

6. You look tired. Why don't you _____ a rest?
　　[take / taking / took]

7. I used to _____ in a convenience store.
　　[work / working / worked]

8. I like _____ dramas on Netflix.
　　[watch / watching / be watched]

9. My bag was _____ last week, so I went to the police.
　　[steal / stole / stolen]

10. If I _____ you, I'd stop smoking.
　　[be / was / were]

❸ Vocabulary

Write the words in the correct spaces. (If necessary, change the verb form.)

crowded	custom	director	holiday	invite
polluted	prefecture	publish	throw away	unique

1. How many people were _____ to the party?

2. The city used to be quite _____, but the air is much cleaner now.

3. Where can I _____ the empty cans and bottles?

4. Venice is a really _____ city. People don't drive cars. They travel by boat everywhere.

5. Taking off your shoes in the house is an important Japanese _____.

6. Is Christmas Day a national _____ in your country?

7. Akira Kurosawa was a famous Japanese movie _____.

8. There were too many people at Universal Studios. I don't like _____ places.

9. Fukushima _____ is in the Tohoku region.

10. This textbook is _____ by Sanshusha.

❹ Writing I

Write the sentences in the correct order.

1. a question / if / the teacher / please / have / you / ask

_____.

2. do / graduation / do / you / want / what / to / after

_____?

3. funny / who / people / like / I / are

_____.

4. do / shall / we / tonight / what

_____?

5. live / Tokyo / used to / in / she

_____.

6. I / should / what / do

_____?

7. going / about / how / the dentist / to

_____?

8. Picasso / by / *Guernica* / painted / was

_____.

9. shoes / take / please / here / off / your

_____.

10. the tallest / Yuriko / used to / in / class / be / girl / her

_____.

⑤ Writing II

Write a question or sentence that matches each answer.

1. A: _____.

B: Married? I don't know. Maybe.

2. A: _____?

B: Terrible. I have a headache and a fever.

3. A: _____?

B: Won the lottery? I don't know. Maybe I'd buy a big house in the country.

4. A: _____?

B: Tomorrow? Why don't we just go to the park and relax?

5. A: _____?

B: Sapporo? About one million, I think.

6. A: _____?

B: I think you should see *Kinkakuji* and *Kiyomizu* temple.

7. A: _____?

B: Your bag? That's terrible! Why don't you call the police?

8. A: _____?

B: An *izakaya* is a kind of restaurant where you can eat and drink.

6 Comprehension

Read the guide to *Todaiji* Temple, Nara Park. Answer the questions with complete sentences.

Todaiji Temple, Nara Park

Todaiji, which means Great Eastern Temple, is one of Japan's most famous temples. It was built in 752 and the *Daibutsuden* (Big Buddha Hall) used to be the world's largest wooden building. Inside the *Daibutsuden* we can see Japan's largest bronze Buddha.

Nara Park is also known for its deer. They make Nara unique. Tourists enjoy feeding them *shika senbei*. Be careful! Many tourists are bitten by the deer every year.

Todaiji is located in the northern part of Nara Park. It is about a 30-minute walk from Kintetsu Station. *Todaiji* and Nara Park are very popular with tourists, so it can become crowded. The best time to visit is early morning if you want to enjoy this picturesque and peaceful place.

1. What does *Todaiji* mean?

2. When was the temple built?

3. Is the *Daibutsuden* the biggest wooden building in the world?

4. What makes Nara unique?

5. Why should tourists be careful?

6. How do you say deer in Japanese?

7. Where in Nara is *Todaiji* located?

_____

8. How far is *Todaiji* from Kintetsu Nara Station?

_____

9. Why does *Todaiji* become crowded?

_____

10. What should you do if you want to visit *Todaiji* when it is quiet?

_____

Unit **1** ［Part A］ ⬥**5**▶**Pair Dictation** (Page 18)

Exercise **1**

Dictate the following sentences to your partner.

次の英文を読み上げて、パートナーに書き取ってもらいなさい。

> John wishes he had more time. If he weren't so busy, he would spend more time with his girlfriend. Now he has to do his part-time job every day.

Exercise **2**

Now listen and write down what your partner says.

今度はあなたがパートナーの言ったことを書き取りなさい。

Exercise **1**

Dictate the following sentences to your partner.

(41)

> Tom wasn't very healthy, but after getting married and having a child, he decided to quit smoking. Now he goes to the gym three times a week and plays futsal at the weekend.

Exercise **2**

Now listen and write down what your partner says.

Unit 3 [Part A] ⑤ Pair Dictation (Page 39)

Exercise 1

Dictate the following sentence to your partner.

Richard used to work for a big company. He had to work long hours and when he got home his children were always asleep. He quit that job and started his own business. Now he is still busy, but he works from home.

Exercise 2

Now listen and write down what your partner says.

Exercise 1

<u>Student A</u>

Can you find the seven changes in John without looking at your partner's picture?

<u>Hint:</u>

A: In my picture John is overweight. How about in your picture?

B: No, in my picture he looks fit.

e.g.   John used to <u>be overweight</u>, but now he <u>is fit</u>.

Memo

· *John used to <u>be overweight</u>, but now he <u>is fit</u>.*

·

·

·

·

·

Turn back to page 41. Write seven sentences in Exercise 2.

Picture A: John, two years ago

Exercise **1**

Dictate the following sentences to your partner.

> The Mona Lisa was painted by Leonardo da Vinci between 1503 and 1506. It can be seen in the Louvre Museum in Paris, France. It is probably the most famous painting in the world.

Exercise **2**

Now listen and write down what your partner says.

_____

_____

_____

_____

_____

Unit 5 [Part A] 5 Pair Dictation (Page 71)

| Exercise 1 ———————————————————————

Dictate the following sentences to your partner.

47

Istanbul is a historic city in Turkey. It is known as the city where East meets West, so it is cosmopolitan. Some people think it is the capital city, but it is not. That is Ankara.

| Exercise 2 ———————————————————————

Now listen and write down what your partner says.

_____

_____

_____

_____

_____

Student A

Exercise 2

You want to find out about the city Miami, Florida. Ask your partner and complete the following table. Use "Key Point Shadowing" or Classroom English when you do not understand.

Miami, Florida	
1. Location	
2. Population	
3. Weather	
4. Industry	
5. Nickname	

Exercise 3

Now listen to your partner and answer their questions about Chicago.

Chicago, Illinois	
1. Location	most southern point of Lake Michigan
2. Population	2.7 million
3. Weather	cold winters, windy
4. Industry	industrial, manufacturing, 20th largest economy in the world
5. Nickname	windy city

Unit 6 [Part A] ⑤ Pair Dictation (Page 80)

Exercise 1

Dictate the following sentences to your partner.

In Chile it is bad manners to pick up food with your hands. You should always use a knife and fork. This is true even if you eat a sandwich. Of course, you can use a spoon to eat soup.

Exercise 2

Now listen and write down what your partner says.

For student **B**

Unit **1** ［Part A］ ❺ **Pair Dictation** (Page 18)

Exercise **1**

Listen and write down what your partner says.

読み上げられた英文を書き取りなさい。

_____

_____

_____

_____

_____

Exercise **2**

Now dictate the following sentences to your partner.

今度は、あなたが次の英文を読み上げて、書き取ってもらいなさい。

Sarah wants to work in Tokyo after graduating. Before starting work, she is going to travel to Europe with her best friend from university.

Exercise 1

Listen and write down what your partner says.

_____

_____

_____

_____

_____

Exercise 2

Now dictate the following sentences to your partner.

Yuna is good at soccer. She would like to be a professional soccer player one day. However, she broke her ankle this year, so she cannot practice. Her coach said she should stay home and rest for a month.

Unit **3** [Part A] ⑤▶**Pair Dictation** (Page 39)

|Exercise 1

Listen and write down what your partner says.

|Exercise 2

Now dictate the following sentence to your partner

Jenny didn't use to be very talkative. At school she was very shy and only had a few friends. She is much more outgoing now. She belongs to the English club at university and entered a speech contest last year.

Exercise 1

Student B

Can you find the seven changes in John without looking at your partner's picture?

Hint:

A: In my picture John is slim and fit. How about in your picture?

B: No, in my picture he looks overweight.

e.g.   John didn't use to be slim and fit, but now he is.

Memo

· *John didn't use to be slim and fit, but now he is.*

·

·

·

·

·

·

Turn back to page 41. Write seven sentences in Exercise 2.

Picture B: John, now

Exercise **1**

Listen and write down what your partner says.

_____

_____

_____

_____

_____

Exercise **2**

Now dictate the following sentences to your partner.

Softbank was founded by Masayoshi Son in 1981. Son was only twenty-four years old when he started the company. Now it is one of the most successful companies in Japan.

Unit 5 [Part A] 5 Pair Dictation (Page 71)

Exercise 1

Listen and write down what your partner says.

Exercise 2

Now dictate the following sentences to your partner.

Honolulu is the world's most remote city. It is 2,300 miles from San Francisco, the nearest major city. However, about 10 million tourists visit Honolulu every year, so it can be crowded.

Student B

Exercise **2**

Listen to your partner and answer their questions about Miami.

Miami, Florida	
1. Location	most southern point of Florida, on the coast
2. Population	metropolitan area, 6.1 million, cosmopolitan
3. Weather	warm climate, mild winters
4. Industry	tourism, entertainment
5. Nickname	magic city

Exercise **3**

You want to find out about the city Chicago, Illinois. Ask your partner and complete the following table. Use "Key Point Shadowing" or Classroom English when you do not understand.

Chicago, Illinois	
1. Location	
2. Population	
3. Weather	
4. Industry	
5. Nickname	

Unit 6 [Part A] 5 Pair Dictation (Page 80)

Exercise 1

Listen and write down what your partner says.

_____

_____

_____

_____

_____

Exercise 2

Now dictate the following sentences to your partner.

> In Russia you should never put your hands in your pockets. That is bad manners. Also, if you make the okay sign with your hand, people will not understand. It is not used in Russia.

Glossary for Reception
（理解のための語彙）

テキストにある英文の内容を理解するのに必要と思われる語彙をアルファベット順に一覧できるようにしました。意味がわからない時に利用してください。

A

a bit of a ～	やや～の素質のある
abroad	海外へ、海外で
accident	事故
active	活動的な
actor	俳優
actually	実際に
add	加える
adjective	形容詞
adult	大人
adverb	副詞
aim	目的
air-conditioner	エアコン
alarm clock	目覚し時計
alcoholic	アルコールの
ambitious	野心のある
Ankara	アンカラ
ankle	足首
anytime	いつでも
appropriate	適切な
arrest	逮捕する
artwork	芸術品
ash	灰
asleep	眠って
athlete	運動選手
athletic	敏捷な、活発な
attribute	属性、性質
avoid	避ける

B

back	背中
bad luck	不運
bandage	包帯
bank	銀行
barbecue	バーベキュー
battery	電池
battle	戦い
be located	位置する

be taken ill	病気になる
beat	打ち負かす
bike	自転車
bitten	bite（噛みつく）の過去分詞形
blow	吹きつける
board game	ボードゲーム（チェス、オセロなど）
boring	退屈な
boss	上司
bowl	鉢、椀
branch	支店、支社
brass band	ブラスバンド
break	（骨を）折る
bring in	取り入れる
broadcast	放送する
bronze	青銅の
bubble period	バブル期
buckwheat	蕎麦
Buddha	仏像
Burgundy	バーガンディ
businessman	ビジネスマン
by the time ～	～の時まで

C

cancel	取り消す
capital	首都、県庁所在地
celebrate	祝う
cellphone	携帯電話
Centrair	セントレア、中部国際空港
ceramics	陶磁器
ceremony	儀式
chain	連鎖店、チェーン
character	登場人物
chess	チェス
Chile	チリ
clean up	きれいに清掃する
clearly	明確に、はっきりと
climate	天候

close down	閉鎖する	direct	監督する
clothes	衣服	directly	直接的に
coach	コーチ	director	監督
coast	沿岸、海岸	disagree	意見が合わない
Columbus	コロンブス	disappointed	がっかりして
come true	実現する	discover	発見する
competitive	競争好きな	dislike	嫌いである
complete	完成する	do ～ a favor	～の願いをきく
complicated	複雑な	dodgeball	ドッジボール
conditional	条件を表す	dorm	寮（dormitory）
Congratulations!	おめでとう！	drawing	スケッチ、デッサン
connect	結びつける、つなぐ		
content word	内容語		

E

continent	大陸
continue	続ける
convenience store	コンビニ
conversely	逆に

earache	耳の痛み
earn	稼ぐ
earthquake	地震
eastern	東の、東に
corner	角	effect	効果
correct	正しい	elementary school	小学校
correctly	正しく	employee	従業員
cosmopolitan	国際的な	empty	空の
cough	咳	end-of-year party	忘年会
counselor	カウンセラー	entertainment	娯楽
countdown	秒読み、カウントダウン	entrance	入口、玄関
create	創造する	episode	エピソード、1つの話
creative	創造的な	era	時代
cross off	線を引いて消す	erupt	噴火する
crowded	混雑した	especially	とりわけ、特に
current	現在の	Europe	ヨーロッパ
custom	慣習	event	出来事、行事
cute	かわいい	excellent	優秀な
		exchange	交換する
		exchange student	交換留学生

D

days	時代
dead	（電気が）なくなった
decline	断る

exciting	わくわくさせる
exercise	運動する
explanation	説明

F

decoration	装飾物、飾り
deer	鹿
definitely	確実に

f.	女性（female）
fantasy	空想の；ファンタジー
deliver	配達する	fascinating	魅力的な
dentist	歯医者	favorite	大好きな；お気に入り
depending on ～	～によって、応じて	feed	えさを与える
depressed	気落ちした	Ferrari	フェラーリ
describe	記述する、述べる	ferry	フェリー
design	デザインする	festival	祭り
dictate	書取らせる		

fever	発熱		Illinois	イリノイ州
fiancé	フィアンセ、婚約者		improve	改善する
figure	姿、人物		in addition	加えて、さらに
film	撮影する		in addition to 〜	〜に加えて
Florida	フロリダ州		in turn	順番に
fluently	流暢に		include	含む
following	次の		industrial	産業が盛んな
for the first time	初めて		industry	産業
fortune	幸運		infinitive	不定詞
found	創設する		influenza	インフルエンザ
full-time	専任の、常勤の		information	情報
functional	機能的な		injure	負傷させる
funny	おかしい		input	入れる
futsal	フットサル		inside	〜の中に
			insomnia	不眠症
G			invent	発明する
galaxy	銀河		iPhone	アイフォン
garbage	ゴミ		Istanbul	イスタンブール
gerund	動名詞			
get divorced	離婚する		**J**	
glasses	メガネ		junior high school	中学校
graduate	卒業する			
graduation	卒業		**K**	
grammatical	文法的な		kindergarten	幼稚園
greet	挨拶する		knee	膝
greeting	挨拶			
guess	推測する、当てる		**L**	
Guggenheim Museum　グッゲンハイム美術館			Lamborghini	ランボルギーニ
guide	指導する		lasagna	ラザーニャ
			lazy	怠惰な
H			least	最も少なく
hang	掛ける、掛けて飾る		Leonardo da Vinci	レオナルド・ダ・ビンチ
hang out	外に干す		lifestyle	生活様式
hardworking	勤勉な		likely	〜しそうな
healthy	健康的な		lively	活気に満ちた
high-tech	ハイテクの		Liverpool	リバプール
historic, historical	歴史的な		local	地域の
Honolulu	ホノルル		location	位置
huge	巨大な、莫大な		Long time no see.	お久し振りです。
hurt	痛む		lose weight	減量する
hypothetical	仮定の		lottery	宝くじ
			Louvre Museum	ルーブル美術館
I				
ideal	理想的な		**M**	
identify	結びつける、確認する		m.	男性(male)
if necessary	必要なら		magic	魔法；魅惑的な

major	大きい、主要な
manufacturing	製造業の
married	結婚して
martial art	格闘技
masterpiece	傑作
medicine	薬
memorize	覚える、暗記する
messy	散らかった
metropolitan	主要都市の
mild	温和な
million	100万
millions of ～	何百万の～
mind	気にする
movie theater	映画館
mural	壁画
musical	音楽好きの

N

natural	自然な
naughty	腕白な
negative	否定的な
nervous	神経質な
Netflix	ネットフリックス
New Year's Eve	大晦日
noisy	騒がしい
noodle	麺類
normal	普通の
northern	北の
note	注、注目する
notes	メモ、覚え書
noticeboard	掲示板
novel	小説

O

object	目的語
on one's own	ひとりで
once	いったん～したら
original	独自の
outgoing	外交的な
overtime	超過勤務、時間外で
overweight	太り過ぎの、肥満
own	所有する
Oxford	オックスフォード

P

P.E.（physical education）体育

Pablo Picasso	パブロ・ピカソ
participate	参加する
passage	一節
passive	受け身の；受動態
pasta	パスタ
pattern	模様
pause	休む、間をおく
peaceful	平和な
perfectly	完璧に
period	時代
personality	性格
philosopher	哲学者、賢人
phrasal verb	句動詞
picturesque	絵のように美しい
plate	皿
point	端
polite	礼儀正しい
polluted	汚染された
popular	人気のある
population	人口
positive	肯定的な
possible	可能な
post	掲示物をはる
pot	つぼ、かめ
pray	祈る
predict	予測する
prediction	予測
prefecture	県
prefer	好む
prepare	準備する
prime minister	首相
pronounce	発音する
professional	プロの
pronoun	代名詞
publish	出版する
put away	片付ける
put on	身に付ける
put up	掲示する、取り付ける
put up with ～	～を我慢する

Q

| quit | やめる |

R

| raise | あげる |
| reason | 理由 |

rebellion	反乱、暴動	substitution	置き換え
recently	最近	suitable	適した、ふさわしい
recommend	勧める、推奨する	sweet potato	サツマイモ
region	地域	switch	スイッチを切り換える
release	公開する、放つ	syllable	音節
remote	遠隔の、へんぴな		
rental store	レンタル店	**T**	
reply	返事：答える	take a break	休憩する
retire	退職する	take a look	一見する
review	復習する	Take care!	では！じゃ、お大事に！
robbery	強盗事件	take off	脱ぐ、はずす
role	役割	take out	取り出す、持ち出す
rule	規則、ルール	take part in ～	～に参加する
Russia	ロシア	take turns	交替でする
		talkative	おしゃべりな
S		tell off	ひどく叱る
samurai warrior	侍	temperature	体温、温度
San Francisco	サンフランシスコ	temple	寺
sandwich	サンドイッチ	tense	時制
science fiction	空想科学小説	term	言葉
sculpture	彫刻	terrible	猛烈な、恐ろしい
self	自己、自分自身	the flu	インフルエンザ
separate	別個の、独立した	these days	近頃では
series	シリーズ	throw away	捨てる
shared	共用の	tidy up	整頓する、片付ける
shorten	短くする	time travel	タイムトラベル,時空旅行する
shrine	神社	title	表題をつける
shy	恥ずかしがりの	tour	旅行
similar	似ている	tourism	観光産業
simple	簡単な	tourist	旅行者
situation	状況	touristy	観光客でにぎわう
smart	利口な	traditional	伝統的な
smartphone	スマホ	translate	翻訳する
social studies	社会科	trash	ゴミ
soup	スープ	trumpet	トランペット
southern	南の	try on	着てみる
southwest	南西(の)	Turkey	トルコ
space	宇宙、余白	turn down	(音量を)下げる
sports day	運動会	turn to page ～	～ページを開く
sprain	くじく、捻挫する	twist	ひねる
spread	広がる	typhoon	台風
stand	我慢する	typical	典型的な
Starbucks	スターバックス	typically	典型的に
straight away	すぐに		
subject	科目、主語	**U**	
substitute	置き換える	ugly	醜い

unique	ユニークな、独特の
unlikely	ありそうもない
usually	通常、普通は

V

Venice	ベニス
volunteer	ボランティア
volcano	火山

W

wallet	財布
washing	洗濯物
weather	天気

website	ウェブサイト
while	一方
windy	風の強い
wooden	木製の
work overtime	超過勤務する
World Heritage Site	世界遺産
worrier	思い悩む人
worry	心配する
wrap	包む、巻きつける

Y

YouTube	ユーチューブ

Glossary for Production
（発話のための語彙）

ペアで活動する際に役立つと思われる語彙について、トピック別にあるいは下位項目毎にアイウエオ順にまとめてみました（**7**の性格描写については、対となる反意語とともに示してあります。また、**3**の年中行事・国民の祝日は、1月より順に整理してあります）。日本語に相当する英語がわからない時に活用してください。

■ 将来の職業（Future Jobs）
（1）職種（Types of Jobs）

アナウンサー	announcer
～員	～ worker
インストラクター	instructor
ウェイター	waiter / server
ウェイトレス	waitress / server
受付係	receptionist
会計士	accountant
会社員	office worker, company employee
会社経営者	office manager
カウンセラー	counselor
外交官	diplomat
看護師	nurse
教師	teacher
客室乗務員	flight attendant
銀行員	bank clerk
警察官	police officer
警備員	security guard
建築家	architect
芸術家	artist
芸人	entertainer
公務員	government worker, government official, civil servant, bureaucrat
コピーライター	copywriter
作家	writer, novelist
サラリーマン	salaried worker
自営業者	self-employed, store owner, restaurant owner, shopkeeper
歯科医	dentist
仕立屋、洋服屋	tailor
ジャーナリスト	journalist
写真家	photographer
修理工、整備工	mechanic
消防士	fire fighter
政治家	politician, statesman
声優	voice actor
僧侶	Buddhist priest
大工	carpenter
タレント	TV personality
調理師、板前	cook, chef
通訳	interpreter
ディスクジョッキー	disc jockey
デザイナー	designer
店員	clerk, salesperson
添乗員	tour conductor
電気技師	electrician
天気予報士	weather forecaster
ニュースキャスター	anchorman, anchorwoman
庭師	gardener
農業従事者	farmer
花屋	florist
パイロット	pilot
パン屋	baker
美容師	hairdresser
不動産業	real estate agent
宝石商	jeweler
翻訳家	translator
漫画家	cartoonist
めがね商	optician
モデル	model
薬剤師	pharmacist
郵便集配人	mailman
理容師	barber
旅行業者	travel agent

（2）勤め先（Workplaces）

学校	school
学習塾	cram school / *juku*
ガソリンスタンド	gas station
銀行	bank

結婚式場	wedding hall	掃除する	clean
工場	factory	将来役立つ	(be) useful for the future
コンサートホール	concert hall	注文を取る	take orders
コンビニ	convenience store	〜の責任がある	(be) responsible for 〜
食料雑貨店	grocery store	（〜から〜まで）働く	work from 〜 to / until 〜
書店	bookshop	良い経験になる	(be) a good experience
ジム	gym		

商社	trading company
スポーツ・センター	sports center
専門学校	technical school
大学	college, university
デパート	department store
〜 店	〜 store / shop
バー	bar
100円ショップ	100-yen shop
ファーストフード・レストラン	
	fast-food restaurant
ファミリー・レストラン	family restaurant
保育所、保育園	nursery school
保険会社	insurance company
レジャー・ランド	amusement park
郵便局	post office
幼稚園	kindergarten

（3）その他（Other）

客	customer
勤務時間	working hours
勤務条件	working conditions
経験	experience
時間給	hourly pay / wage
職務	duties
上司	boss
係長	chief
課長	department head
部長	manager
営業部長	business manager
副社長	vice-president
社長	president
制服	uniform
賃金	pay / salary
同僚	co-worker
マネージャー	manager
面接	interview
給仕する	serve
仕事を探す	look for a job
仕事を辞める	quit a job

2 趣味／娯楽（Hobbies / Pastimes）

アニメ	animation
編物	knitting
インターネット	the Internet
ウェート・トレーニング	weight training
エアロビクス	aerobics
絵画	painting
格闘技	martial arts
楽器	musical instrument
カラオケ	singing karaoke
切手収集	stamp collecting
キャンプ	camping
ギャンブル	gambling
コンピュータおたく	computer freak
サーフィン	surfing
サイクリング	cycling
魚釣り	fishing
小説	novel
ジョギング	jogging
推理小説	mystery
スキー	skiing
スケート	skating
スノーボード	snowboarding
ダイビング	scuba diving
ドライブ	driving
ハイキング	hiking
ビデオゲーム	video games
ボーリング	bowling
漫画	comic book
ヨット遊び	sailing
料理	cooking

3 買い物／年中行事／日本の祝日
（Shopping / Annual Events / Japanese Holidays）
（1）買い物（Shopping）

衣料品店	clothing store
おもちゃ	toy
家具	furniture
眼鏡店	optician's

携帯電話	cellular phone
健康食品店	health food shop
雑貨店	variety shop
ショッピングセンター	shopping mall
スーパー	supermarket
スポーツ用品	sporting goods
地下街	underground mall, underground shopping arcade
中古品店	thrift shop
デリカテッセン	delicatessen
電気製品	appliance
電子辞書	electronic dictionary
のみの市	flea market
パン屋	bakery
美術工芸品	arts and crafts
ブティック	boutique
ブランド品	brand-name goods
古本屋	secondhand bookshop
文房具	stationary
宝石	jewelry
みやげ物店	gift shop
安売り店	discount shop

（2）年中行事 （Annual Events）

正月休み	New Year's holidays
（節分の）豆まき	Bean-throwing Ceremony
バレンタインデー	Valentine's Day
ひな祭	The Dolls' Festival
花見	cherry blossom viewing
ゴールデン・ウィーク	Golden Week
メーデー	May Day
お中元	summer / mid-year gift
七夕	The Star Festival
お盆	All Soul's Festival
花火（大会）	fireworks
盆踊り	Bon Festival dance
月見	moon viewing
ハロウィーン	Halloween
お歳暮	winter / year-end gift
クリスマス休暇	Christmas holidays
大晦日	New Year's Eve

（3）日本の祝日 （Japanese Holidays）

国民の祝日	national holidays
元日	New Year's Day
成人の日	Coming of Age Day, Adult's Day
建国記念の日	National Foundation Day
天皇誕生日	The Emperor's Birthday
春分の日	Vernal Equinox Day
昭和の日	Showa Day
憲法記念日	Constitution Memorial Day
みどりの日	Greenery Day
こどもの日	Children's Day
海の日	Marine Day
山の日	Mountain Day
敬老の日	Respect for the Aged Day
秋分の日	Autumnal Equinox Day
スポーツの日	Sports Day
文化の日	Culture Day
勤労感謝の日	Labor Thanksgiving Day

4 旅行／観光地 （Travel / Famous Places in Japan and Overseas to Visit）
（1）旅行の種類と旅行先 （Kinds of Travel, Destinations）

温泉地	hot spring resort
海外旅行	overseas trip
海水浴	sea bathing
観光旅行	sightseeing trip
記念館	memorial
記念碑	monument
研修旅行	study tour
史跡	historical site
植物園	botanical garden
城	castle
神社	shrine
水族館	aquarium
卒業旅行	graduation trip
寺	temple
展望台	observatory
動物園	zoo
２泊３日の旅行	three-day trip
博物館	museum
日帰り旅行	day trip
美術館	art gallery
見晴らし台	scenic lookout
遊園地	amusement park

(2) 観光地 (Famous Places to Visit)

エアーズ・ロック	Ayer's Rock
英仏海峡トンネル	The "Chunnel"
エッフェル搭	The Eiffel Tower
エンパイア・ステート・ビル	The Empire State Building
グランド・キャニオン	The Grand Canyon
ゴールデン・ゲイト・ブリッジ	The Golden Gate Bridge
コロセウム	The Colosseum
自由の女神	The Statue of Liberty
スカイツリー	Tokyo Skytree
タージ・マハル	The Taj Mahal
東京ディズニーランド	Tokyo Disneyland
ナイアガラの滝	Niagara Falls
長島スパーランド	Nagashima Spa Land
ノートルダム寺院	Notre Dame Cathedral
パナマ運河	The Panama Canal
万里の長城	The Great Wall of China
ヒマラヤ山脈	The Himalayas
ピラミッド	The Pyramids
広島平和記念資料館	Hiroshima Peace Memorial Museum
ユニバーサル・スタジオ・ジャパン	Universal Studios Japan
ルーブル美術館	The Louvre
ワシントン記念搭	The Washington Monument

5 結婚 (Marriage)

ウェディング・ドレス	wedding dress / gown
結婚式	wedding ceremony
結婚の誓い	wedding vows
結婚披露宴	wedding reception
婚約	engagement
婚約する	get engaged
新婚旅行	honeymoon trip
神前結婚式	Shinto ceremony
仲人	go-between, matchmaker
花婿	bridegroom
花嫁	bride
フィアンセ	fiancé, fiancée
プロポーズする	propose, ask for her hand in marriage
見合い結婚	arranged marriage
結納金	betrothal money

洋式結婚式	western style wedding
恋愛結婚	love marriage
和式結婚式	traditional Japanese wedding

6 健康問題 (Health and Disease)
(1) 病名・症状 (Names of Disease, Symptoms)

胃痛	stomachache
悪寒	chill
花粉症	hay fever
筋肉痛	muscle pain
下痢	diarrhea
歯痛	toothache
耳痛	earache
消化不良	indigestion
食欲不振	loss of appetite
じんましん	hives
咳	cough
ぜんそく	asthma
食べ過ぎ	overeating
熱がある	have a fever
捻挫(する)	sprain
のどの痛み	sore throat
肺炎	pneumonia
吐き気	nausea
吐き気がする	nauseous
鼻水	runny nose
微熱	slight fever
貧血	anemia
不眠症	insomnia
水虫	athlete's foot
むかつき(胃の不調)	upset stomach
胸やけ	heartburn
目の乾き	dry eye
めまい	dizziness
腰痛	lower-back pain

(2) 薬 (Medicine)

胃薬	stomach medicine
風邪薬	cold medicine
解熱薬	fever reducer
下痢止め薬	antidiarrheal
鎮静薬	sedative
鎮痛薬	painkiller
目薬	eye drops

（3）その他 (Other)

眼科	eye clinic	小児科	pediatrics
救急救命室	ER / emergency room	整形外科	orthopedics
救急車	ambulance	食べ過ぎ	overeating
外科	surgery	内科	internal medicine
症状	symptom	副作用	side effect
食欲をなくす	lose appetite	薬局	pharmacy

7 性格描写 (Words to Describe Character / Personality)

荒っぽい	rough	優しい	tender
粋な	stylish	ださい	unfashionable
思いやりのある	considerate	思いやりがない	inconsiderate
面白味のある	interesting	つまらない	dull
かっこいい	cool	風変わりな	weird
頑固な	stubborn	素直な	flexible
寛大な	generous	けちな	stingy
協力的な	helpful	非協力的な	uncooperative
勤勉な	hardworking	怠惰な	lazy
こぎれいな	neat	だらしのない	sloppy
才能豊かな	gifted	無能な	untalented
社交的な	outgoing	内気な	shy
正直な	honest	不正直な	dishonest
親切な	kind	冷酷な	cruel
信頼のおける	reliable	当てにならない	unreliable
清潔な	clean	乱雑な	messy
誠実な	sincere	偽善的な	insincere
精力的な	energetic	無気力な	inactive
多忙な	busy	暇な	idle
頼りになる	dependable	頼りにならない	undependable
知的な	intelligent	無学の	ignorant
忠実な	loyal	不誠実な	disloyal
人なつっこい	friendly	よそよそしい	aloof
人を楽しませる	amusing	活気のない	lifeless
ひょうきんな	funny	たいくつな	boring
誇らしげな	proud	控え目な	humble
真面目な	serious	こっけいな	comical
魅力的な	attractive	魅力のない	unattractive
もの静かな	quiet	騒がしい	loud
礼儀正しい	polite	無作法な	rude, impolite

著　者
Julyan Nutt（ジュリアン・ナット）東海学園大学
Michael Marshall（マイケル・マーシャル）東海学園大学
倉橋洋子（くらはし ようこ）東海学園大学名誉教授
宮田学（みやた まなぶ）名古屋市立大学名誉教授

コミュニケーションのための実践英語4 [中級編]

2020 年 9 月 20 日　　第 1 版発行
2022 年 9 月 20 日　　第 2 版発行

著　　者──Julyan Nutt / Michael Marshall / 倉橋洋子 /
　　　　　　宮田学
発 行 者──前田俊秀
発 行 所──株式会社 三修社
　　　　　　〒150-0001東京都渋谷区神宮前2-2-22
　　　　　　TEL 03-3405-4511　FAX 03-3405-4522
　　　　　　振替 00190-9-72758
　　　　　　https://www.sanshusha.co.jp
　　　　　　編集担当 三井るり子
印 刷 所──港北メディアサービス株式会社

©2020 Printed in Japan ISBN978-4-384-33500-2 C1082

表紙デザイン──峯岸孝之
本文デザイン・DTP──株式会社 明昌堂
本文イラスト──パント大吉
準拠音声録音──ELEC(吹込み：Neil DeMaere / Carolyn Milller / Rachel Walzer)
準拠音声制作──高速録音株式会社

教科書準拠CD発売
本書の準拠CDをご希望の方は弊社までお問い合わせください。